First World War
and Army of Occupation
War Diary
France, Belgium and Germany

20 DIVISION
Divisional Troops
Divisional Trench Mortar Batteries
24 May 1916 - 30 January 1919

WO95/2106/2

The Naval & Military Press Ltd
www.nmarchive.com
Published in association with The National Archives

Published by

The Naval & Military Press Ltd

Unit 10 Ridgewood Industrial Park,

Uckfield, East Sussex,

TN22 5QE England

Tel: +44 (0) 1825 749494

www.naval-military-press.com

www.nmarchive.com

This diary has been reprinted in facsimile from the original. Any imperfections are inevitably reproduced and the quality may fall short of modern type and cartographic standards.

© **Crown Copyright**
Images reproduced by permission of The National Archives, London, England, 2015.

Contents

Document type	Place/Title	Date From	Date To
Heading	2106/2		
Heading	20th Division Divl Artillery Divl Trench Mortars May 1916-Feb 1919		
Heading	20 D.A.C. Vol 8		
Miscellaneous	59th Light Trench Mortar Battery.		
Miscellaneous	Honour & Awards-59th Light T.M. Bty.		
Miscellaneous	Officers Killed In action while rebury with 59th L.T.M.B.	00/03/1918	00/03/1918
Miscellaneous			
Miscellaneous	20 Div Arty Trench Mortar Brigade History Commanding On The 10.4.1917	10/04/1917	10/04/1917
Miscellaneous			
Miscellaneous	Beer a/c.		
Miscellaneous			
Heading	War Diary 20th Divisional Artillery Trench Mortar Brigade 24.5.16 to 30.6.16 Feb 19 Vol 1 + 2		
War Diary	In The Field On 20 Divn. Fronts Viz	24/05/1916	24/05/1916
War Diary	C.22. Central to I.11.d.10.0	24/05/1916	02/06/1916
War Diary	Field.	03/06/1916	01/07/1916
Heading	War Diary 20th Divisional Artillery Trench Mortar Brigade. July (27.7.16-31.7.16) 1916		
War Diary	Field.	07/07/1916	17/07/1916
Heading	20th Divisional Artillery. 20th Division Trench Mortar Brigade August 1916		
Heading	War Diary Of 20th Divl Arty Trench Mortars August 1916 Volume VI. Vol 8.		
War Diary	Ypres.	30/07/1916	09/08/1916
War Diary	Field.	10/08/1916	01/09/1916
Heading	20th Divisional Artillery. 20th Division Trench Mortar Brigade September 1916		
Heading	War Diary of the 20th Div Arty Trench Mortar Brigade 1st September 1916 to 30 Sept 1916 Vol 9		
War Diary	Field.	01/09/1916	14/09/1916
Heading	20th Divisional Artillery. 20th Division Trench Mortar Brigade October 1916		
Heading	War Diary for October 1916 Trench Mortars 20th Division Artillery Vol 10		
War Diary	Field.	01/10/1916	31/10/1916
Heading	20th Divisional Artillery. 20th Division Trench Mortar Brigade November 1916		
Heading	War Diary For Nov 1st to 30th 1916 20th Divl Artillery Trench Mortars Vol XI		
War Diary	Field.	01/11/1916	30/11/1916
Heading	20th Divisional Artillery 20th Division Trench Mortar Brigade December 1916		
Heading	R.A. Trench Mortars. 20th Division War Diary December 1916 Vol 12		
War Diary	Field.	01/12/1916	31/12/1916
Heading	War Diary R.A. Trench Mortar 20th Division. Vol 13		
War Diary	Field.	01/01/1917	31/01/1917

Heading	War Diary of the T M Bty 9w Vol 14		
War Diary	Field.	01/02/1917	26/02/1917
Heading	War Diary R.A. Trench Mortar Brigade 20th Division March. 1917 Vol 3. Vol 15		
War Diary	Field.	08/03/1917	29/03/1917
Heading	War Diary R.A. Trench Mortars 20th Division 1st to 30th April 17 (Vol IV)		
War Diary	Field.	08/04/1917	30/04/1917
Heading	War Diary Trench Mortars 20 Division 1st May to 31st May 1917 Vol 17		
War Diary	Field.	03/05/1917	30/05/1917
Heading	War Diary 20th Division Trench Mortar. 1st-30th June 1917 Vol 18		
Heading	War Diary.		
War Diary	Field.	01/06/1917	30/06/1917
Heading	War Diary Of 20th Divl Trench Mortars 1st to 31st July 1917 (Vol 7)		
War Diary	Field.	03/07/1917	31/07/1917
Miscellaneous	Brigade Orders by Captain A.M.G. Lin A.S.A. D.T.M.D. 20th Division.	01/08/1917	01/08/1917
Heading	War Diary R.A. Trench Mortars 20th Divl 1st-31st August, 1917. Vol 20		
War Diary	Field.	01/08/1917	19/08/1917
War Diary	Field.	12/08/1917	31/08/1917
Heading	War Diary Of 20th. Divl. Arty. Trench Mortars. From. 1.9.17 To: 30.9.17. Volume 9		
Heading	War Diary.		
War Diary	Field.	04/09/1917	30/09/1917
Heading	War Diary of 20th Divnl. Arty. Trench Mortars. From 1st October to 31st. October. 1917. Vol 10		
War Diary	Field.	01/10/1917	14/10/1917
War Diary	Field.	03/10/1917	30/10/1917
Heading	War Diary of Trench Mortars 20th Divl Arty From 1st Nov 17 to 30th Nov 17 Vol 11		
War Diary	Fins (area)	01/11/1917	10/11/1917
War Diary	Field.	11/11/1917	30/11/1917
Heading	War Diary 20th Div Trench Mortars December 1917 (Vol 12)		
War Diary	Field.	01/12/1917	31/12/1917
Heading	War Diary of 20th Div. Arty. Trench Mortars. From 1st Jan 18 to 31 Jan 18 Vol 1.		
War Diary		07/01/1918	31/01/1918
Heading	20th Division. 21. No. Bde. February 1918.		
War Diary	Field.	01/02/1918	28/02/1918
Heading	20th Divisional Artillery. Trench Mortars 20th Division. March 1918		
Heading	War Diary of R.A. Trench Mortars. 20th Divn. From 1st to 31st March 1918 Vol III.		
Miscellaneous	Cover for Documents. Nature of Enclosures.		
War Diary	Field.	04/03/1918	27/03/1918
War Diary	Field.	02/03/1918	02/03/1918
Heading	War Diary of 20th R.A.T. Mortars 1st to 30th April 1918 Vol IV		
War Diary	In The Field.	02/04/1918	30/04/1918
Heading	War Diary of R.A. Trench Mortars 20th Divn 1st to 31st May 1918 Vol V.		

Miscellaneous	Cover for Documents. Nature of Enclosures.		
War Diary	In The Field.	01/05/1918	31/05/1918
Heading	War Diary of 20th R.A. Trench Mortars From 1st to 30th June 1918 Vol VI		
Miscellaneous	Cover for Documents. Nature of Enclosures.		
War Diary	In The Field.	01/06/1918	30/06/1918
Heading	War Diary. of 20th R.A. Trench Mortars. from 1st to 31st July 1918 Vol VII.		
Miscellaneous	Cover for Documents. Nature of Enclosures.		
War Diary	In The Field.	01/07/1918	31/07/1918
Heading	War Diary of 20th R.A. Trench Mortars from 1st to 31st August 1918 Vol VIII.		
Miscellaneous	Cover for Documents. Nature of Enclosures.		
War Diary	In The Field.	01/08/1918	31/08/1918
Heading	War Diary of 20th R.A. Trench Mortars from 1st to 30th Sept 1918 Vol IX		
Miscellaneous	Cover for Documents. Nature of Enclosures.		
War Diary		01/09/1918	30/09/1918
Heading	War Diary of 20th R.A. Trench Mortars. From 1st to 31st October 1918 Vol X		
Miscellaneous	Cover for Documents. Nature of Enclosures.		
War Diary		01/10/1918	31/10/1918
Heading	War Diary of 20th. Divnl. Arty. Trench Mortars. From 1.11.18 to 30.11.18 Vol. XI.		
Miscellaneous	Cover for Documents. Nature of Enclosures.		
War Diary	In The Field.	01/11/1918	30/11/1918
Heading	War Diary of 20th Divnl. Arty. Trench Mortars. from 1.12.18 to 31.12.18. Vol: 12.		
Miscellaneous	Cover for Documents. Nature of Enclosures.		
War Diary	In The Field.	01/12/1918	31/12/1918
Heading	War Diary of 20th Divnl. Arty Trench Mortars. from. 1st Jan. 1919. To. 31st Jan. 1919. Vol: I.		
Miscellaneous	Cover for Documents. Nature of Enclosures.		
War Diary	In The Field.	01/01/1919	30/01/1919
Heading	War Diary of 20th Divnl. Arty. Trench Mortars. From. 1.2.19. To. 28.2.19. Vol: 2.		
Miscellaneous	Cover for Documents. Nature of Enclosures.		
Miscellaneous			

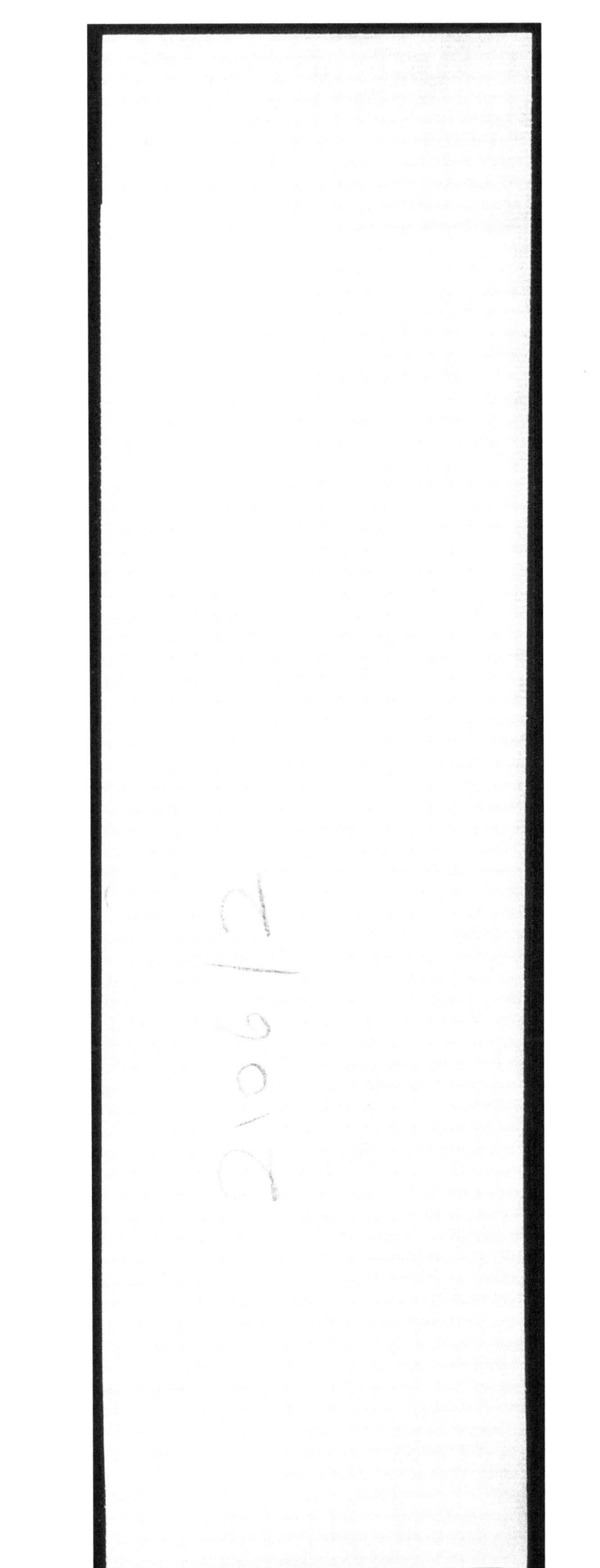

20TH DIVISION
DIVL ARTILLERY

DIVL TRENCH MORTARS
MAY 1916 - FEB 1919

2o D.A.C.
Vol 8

59th Light Trench Mortar Battery.

Battery formed April 1916. under command of 2Lieut (A/Capt)
L.B. DAVIS. 11th K.R.R.C.

Took part in series of raids & demonstrations at YPRES preparatory to SOMME battle during June & July 1916. During raid on night 25/26 June 1916. L/Cpl. J. ROUSFIELD. Rifle Brigade. att'd 59.L.T.M.B. was awarded M.M. for conspicuous gallantry.

Proceeded to SOMME & went into action W. of GUILLEMONT about 22nd Aug't. Carried out most useful work. During local counter attack about 4th Sep. Capt. L.B. DAVIS awarded M.C. for courageous manner in which he commanded his gun which did most effective work & caused numerous casualties to enemy. Battery moved forward with assaulting troops who took the strongly fortified village of GUILLEMONT on 3rd Sept., & continued to fight throughout engagements in which 59th Inf Brigade took part, including the German retirement in March 1917, rendering invaluable assistance to battalions. Lieut S.H. SMITH. Gen. List, att'd 59.L.T.M.B., was mentioned in Despatches & Sgt. A.J. SMART. Rifle Brigade att'd 59.LT.M.B. awarded D.C.M. (January 1917) for excellent work done during SOMME fighting.

Battery went into action at BULLECOURT in June 1917, where enemy mortars were extremely active, & caused numerous casualties & inconvenience to our infantry. Strenuous counter battery work was carried out, & at the end of a week enemy mortars were completely defeated.
Capt. L.B. DAVIS wounded 2-6-17. Lieut (A/Capt). S.H. SMITH. Gen. List, assumed command.
From July 1917 to September 1917 battery took part in fighting in Flanders, & despite difficult circumstances — mud, transport of ammunition etc — maintained its good record. During the battle of the STEENBEKE, Rfman W. FOUNTAIN, Rifle Brigade. att'd 59 L.T.M.B. was awarded the M.M. for great gallantry in rescuing wounded.

Went into action E. of GOUZECOURT in October 1917 & carried out most effective offensive work. Took part in assault of on Nov. 20th & again during enemy counter attack on 30th Nov., where, under most difficult circumstances, the battery played a most effective part.

Normal trench warfare in Flanders until February 1918.
Capt. S.H. SMITH. Gen. List awarded M.C. January 1918.
Sgt. L.B. MORGAN. Rifle Brigade att'd 59 T.M.B. awarded M.S.M. Jan. 1918.
Battery reformed after March Offensive, & went into action W. of LENS May 1918. Carried out useful & effective work, continually supporting

raids & supplying gun detachments to accompany infantry patrols. Special attention was paid to training men in considering the light mortar as a mobile weapon, also use in defence against low flying aircraft were successfully harassed on several occasions.

In September 1918. Cpl. R. BURROUGH. K.R.R.C. attd 59th L.T.M.B. was awarded M.M. for bravery & the manner in which he handled his gun while accompanying a day light patrol. During the fighting near SALLAUMINES & MERICOURT 1st–6th Oct. battery carried out excellent work by accompanying foremost infantry patrols during their advance. During this fighting, 2Lt. T.L. POTTER. Rifle Brigade, attd 59th L.T.M.B. was awarded the M.C. for displaying great bravery & initiative, & rendering invaluable assistance to the infantry by the efficient manner in which he handled his guns.

Honours & Awards – 59th Light T.M. Bty.

M.C.

Captain L.B. DAVIS.   August 1916.
   11th K.R.R.C. att. 59 T.M.B.

~~Captain~~ S.A. SMITH.   January 1918.
Gen. List. ~~11th K.R.R.C.~~ att. 59 T.M.B.

2Lt. T.L. POTTER.   October 1918.
   11th Rifle Brigade. att. 59 T.M.B.

Mention in Despatches.

Lieut. S.A. SMITH.   January. 1917.
   11th K.R.R.C. att. 59 T.M.B.

D.C.M.

~~Cpl. FARRINGTON.~~ ~~June 1916.~~

Sgt. A.J. SMART.
   11th Rifle Brigade. January 1917.

Military Medal.

L/Cpl Mansfield.
   Rifle Brigade.   June 1916.

Rfman F........... W.   August 1917.
   11th Rifle Brigade att. 59 T.M.B.

Cpl. BURROUGH R. September 1918.
   11th K.R.R.C. att. 59 T.M.B.

M.S.M.

Sgt. MORGAN. J.S. – January 1918.
   11th Rifle Brigade att. 59th T.M.B.

Officers killed in action while serving with
59th L.T.M.B.

2nd Lieut E. HORSLEY. K.R.R.C.
　　　　Killed in Action W. of Langemarck.
　　　　　　　　August 1917.

2nd Lieut J. ABBOTT. Rifle Brigade.
　　　　Killed in Action. Langemarck.
　　　　　　　　September 1917.

2nd Lieut. H. J. CAPERN. K.R.R.C.
　　　　Killed in Action. Nr. NESLE.
　　　　　　　　March 1918.

The 20th Div. T.M. Brigade was formed at the beginning of 1916 under the Command of Capt. R. Tailyour. It consisted of three 2 in Batteries X. Y. Z. and one 9.45 Battery V/20. Much useful work was done but the Batteries were handicapped by shortage of personnel up to May, when a large number of men became available owing to the disbandoning of the Brigade Ammunition Columns, when volunteers were called for, and over 150 N.C.O's & men volunteered to fill 79 places in what was then termed as the "Suicide Club" by those who did not belong to it. Needless to say by getting volunteers for the work, men were obtained who had their heart & soul in the job and the use of trench mortars became a great factor in trench warfare.

Capt. Tailyour met with an accident about this time, breaking his leg, and the Command was taken over by Capt. H.B. Buckley.

About the end of May the Division took over the Ypres front from Wieltje to Railway Wood and previously the use of trench mortars was hardly known on this sector. Work was at once started to put in emplacements all along the sector, and a considerable amount of firing was done. Trench Mortars were at this time being used for wire cutting using the very sensitive Newton Fuze. This was found to be a great success and from then onwards the cutting of wire was done mainly by T.M.s. in addition to the usual and daily destroying of enemy trench works.

The Infantry of the Division went South in July 1916 but the Artillery & T.M.s remained behind at Ypres covering alternately the 6th & 29th Division, who had come up from the Somme.

From May until September when the T.Ms were relieved several thousand rounds were fired & between 25 to 30 permanent emplacements put in, including one heavy emplacement from which we were never allowed to fire from, to the great disgust of "V" Battery.

During this time the following officers received the M.C.

  Capt H.B. Buckley   D.T.M.O.
  Capt. C.H. Traill   V/20
  Lt. Scott   X/20.

and several N.C.O's then received the M.M. & one D.C.M. The casualties were not heavy considering the amount of work done.

The Divisional Artillery then proceeded to the Somme and very little opportunity was given to put T.M. into the line, owing to the terrible state of the ground, & the mud it was practically impossible to prepare platforms which would stand being fired from for more than a few rounds. It then became the custom to use the T.M. personnel as fatigue parties for the Field Artillery, on more than one occasion, Batteries were taken away from putting in emplacements and doing their own work to carry out these fatigues. Nearly 40% of the trained personnel of the Div T.M. became casualties on this work including two officers killed.

Eventually several emplacements were put in at Sailly Saillesel, guns & ammunition carried up ready for an attack. The moral of the

T.M. personnel rose high, they were at last to have a chance, their hopes only to be dashed to the ground, by orders coming to hand over to another Division who were coming in for it, and then to hear that the part in the show to be played by T.M.s was cancelled altogether.

Another attempt was made later with some success & two 2 inch were used on Bosnia Salient in front of Morval.

During the whole of the 1916/1917 Winter, it was very disheartening for both Officers & men, as they were not given the chance to make use of what opportunities presented themselves for them to carry out their own work.

20th Div. Hvy. Trench Mortars Brigade History commencing ~~at the~~ 10.4.1917

Capt. Buckley left the Brigade on the 10th of April and Capt. Glen then became acting D.T.M.O. The Brigade remained behind at Combles and did not follow up the advance of the Division until the 15th of April when it moved to Sechelle. The Brigade was under canvas here but the men soon built themselves shacks from wood found in the village. As "No Man's Land" on this front varied from 500 to 2000 yards in depth it was impossible to utilise Trench Mortars and most of the men and some Officers were attached to Field Batteries. A very quiet & pleasant time was spent on this front.

On the 24th of May the Divisional Artillery was relieved by the 42nd Divisional Artillery. Next day the Brigade marched north & encamped close to the Sugar Refinery on the Bapaume - Peronne road. From there an advance party rode up to Noreuil to reconnoitre that part of the front line which we were to take over. The Officers in the Brigade at that time were: D.T.M.O. Capt. Glen

"V" Battery   "X" Battery   "Y" Battery
Capt. J. Diespecker 2/Lt. G. Grant   2/Lt. J. Neill
2/Lt. Murray   2/Lt. Blundell   2/Lt. Coggins
2/Lt. McCarthy

"Z" Battery
2/Lt. J. Barret
2/Lt. A. Vincent.

up of a round of fatigues.

On about the 8th of November we were surprised to get orders to dig about 15 more positions as soon as possible and to get up 100 rounds to all guns. Eight Medium and one Heavy position were started in "Surrey" Ravine a favourite target for a German trench mortar. At that time more positions were dug on the right of Gonnelieu. On the 19th all positions were completed and a certain number on the right were handed over to the 12th Division. Our Brigade manned 14 guns in all. It was only a few days before the attack that we knew what was happening.

At 6 A.M. on the 20th all our positions were manned and ammunition was prepared. At 6.10 A.M. we heard the old tanks lumbering up behind us, and ten minutes later we opened out with the crash of our barrage. The Tanks came ridiculously near some of our positions but got passed us alright. The opening range was about 600 yards and we gradually lifted to 1400 yards firing for about 40 minutes at 3 rounds per minute. There was not much retaliation so we could watch the Tanks disappearing over the crest in front of us followed by our infantry.

We were detailed before the attack to take charge of any serviceable

The next move was to Beugnatre
where it was decided to put the
wagon line.

On the 27th of May the Brigade
relieved the 2nd Australian Trench
Mortar Brigade. The Australians
had no T.M. positions on this
front so work was immediately started
on two positions close to the portion
of the "Hindenburg" line which the
Australians had taken a week
or two before. All work had to
be done at night as the Germans looked
down on that part of the line from two
sides. The Battery in the line lived
in a sunken road leading out of
Noreuil, so it meant a weary walk
of about three miles up to the
trenches every night. Not an easy
task under a load of a couple of
mining faces of timber for mining
frames and with the thought of a
night's digging ahead of you.
The Heavy Battery started work
on a position to the left of the Medium
positions and in the "Hindenburg"
line itself. The "Hindenburg" line
of course was practically flattened
out around this part & could
hardly be distinguished from the
rest of the ground. The surroundings
were exceedingly unpleasant. One
could hardly move without treading
on the body of some poor Australian
and the very hot weather did
not help things.
Two guns were soon in action

Lt. Barret was killed on the Canal
Bank. A great loss to the Brigade.
2/Lt Smith was gassed and a good
proportion of the men were killed or
wounded. We lost some horses in
the wagon line from shelling and
bombing.

On the 1st October we were relieved
by the 4th Divisional Trench Mortars and
on the 20 of October we entrained at
Proven for the Somme. 5 pm next
day we arrived at Peronne and
were taken by lorries to Heudicourt.
On the 23rd Battery Commanders
reconnoitred the line and next
day we relieved the 40 Division.
"Y" Battery took over positions a few
hundred yards north of Villers Plouich.
"X" Battery had positions on Welsh
Ridge and "Z" Battery were in
Gonnelieu. The Heavy Battery
took over two very good positions. One
in Gonnelieu and the other on the
Cambrai Road. They did a good
deal of firing with satisfactory results.
The majority of the positions taken
over were for defence only, so new
ones had to be constructed.
Difficulty in obtaining carrying
parties for ammunition kept down
our firing to a great extent.
The front was very quiet and our
positions were not shelled very much.
The men were in the line continuously
but preferred that life to that out
of the line where the day was made

and our first effort to silence some trench mortars which had been troubling our infantry in this sector met with some success. Our average range was 250 yards.

The Germans were using at that time many "Granatenwerfers" and a few medium "Minenwerfers" and he could make it very uncomfortable when he wanted.

Each Medium Battery had 4 days in the line & 8 days out. Four days was quite enough under those conditions and we were not sorry when we got out of the line.

Our bombs were brought up from a dump near Vaux to Noreuil by wagon and taken up to the positions by infantry carrying parties.

On the 20th June we were relieved by the 62nd Division but they did not take over our positions. We had very few casualties on this tour owing to very good luck.

On the 23rd we marched to Fricourt where we remained for 10 days. A not unwelcome rest but a poor place to spend it in.

Lorries took us to Englebermer and we spent the night there in billets. The first time the unit had been billeted in a village with civilians in it for over 8 months. Our next move was to Thièvres and then to Canettemont near Frévent. We knew fairly well what our destination

we came out of the line. We escaped
Shelling there but were bombed now
& then.

The Brigade went into the line again
on the 14th September and took over
guns from the 38th Division. The wagon
lines was moved close to Elverdinghe
on the Poperinghe road. By the
26th of September we had three
guns in Langemarck. Two of them
in the open behind "Pill Boxes" and
the other behind the remains of a
brick wall. Our Head Quarters were
on the Canal Bank. The Battery in
the line living in Pill Boxes (Rifle's
Farm) close to Langemarck. The
Shelling here was as bad as we
had experienced anywhere. Ammunition
Supply was very difficult. All bombs
had to be carried from the Steenbeek
forward at night.

As Langemarck was shelled
continuously it did not much matter
if our positions were discovered or
not.

The Brigade was equipped by this
time with the 6" Newton Trench Mortar
a great improvement over the old
2" T.M. We had to take these
into action the first time without
any previous instruction on them.
Among targets engaged were:- Langemarck
before it was taken, "Eagle" Trench
and "Goed de Vesten" Farm at ranges
varying from 400 yards to 1400 yards.
Our casualties were fairly heavy

was by this time – The Salient. We had a good idea of what was to happen there also.

At Caëstre we received orders to move straight up to Ypres by lorry and at 7 o'clock on the 6'o ~~July~~ we were dumped down in a field near "Canada" Farm with a few tents & bivouac sheets to sleep under. The Boche kept us ~~awake~~ awake that night by flattening shrapnel over the camp and shelling a dump near us with a 4.2" H.V.

This Brigade and also the 61st Divisional Trench Mortars came under the orders of the D.T.M.O. 38th Division.

Battery commanders reconnoitred the line next day and the following day we marched up to the lines receiving a nasty "strafing" in Elverdinghe as we passed through. There were no vacant dugouts on the Canal Bank so we had to be content with bivouac sheets for head cover and some bushes near "Rivoli" Farm for concealment.

Our task was to dig in four guns per battery in five days to be ready for the preliminary bombardment which was to commence on the on about the 14th July. After working night & day this was accomplished. "X" Battery had four guns in "Harwich" trench, "Y"'s guns were in "Aylmer" trench and "Z" Battery were to the left of "X" & closer to the canal

"V" Battery manned a 9.45" Trench Mortar on the Canal Bank.

As soon as the positions were completed detachments moved up to the guns and lived in trench shelters.

We commenced firing on the 16th July and averaged 200 rounds per day. This was quite good considering our difficulties. The Germans shelled continuously during the night, the only period ammunition could be pushed up the light railway. The railway was never without a few gaps no matter how quickly the R.E's repaired it. Positions were being continually blown in by shell fire which meant many hours work to repair them. The rifle mechanisms gave a great deal of trouble. As there was a shortage of them it kept down our firing a lot. Our job was to cut all the German wire & obliterate their front line. We did not have much difficulty in doing that.

We came out of the line on the 30th of July the day before the 38th Division attacked.

Our casualties were heavy "Z" battery came out with 1 officer one cook and a man. Capt. D. westlake, 2/Lt Murry & 2/Lt Coggins were gassed and 2/Lt Bamford was wounded slightly.

Several premature's made the men's casualty list longer.

Our camp was moved back to a wood near St Sixte a week after

guns captured. A 4.2 howitzer and
several 77mm guns were some found.
These were fired at the Enemy every
day until the 27th when orders were
received to pull them out with limbers
from the D.A.C.
It was proposed to put in a Heavy
Trench Mortar on the Slope South East
of Marcoing. A position was found
but luckily enough for ourselves the
Germans attacked the day we were
to have started work so we were
not affected by his attack very much
although it was rather uncomfortable
in Villers Plouich where the
Brigade was. Havrincourt was
rather too close to the Boche for our
wagon line so our whole camp was
moved to Metz-en-Couture.
On December 5th positions were
reconnoitred to enable us to "strafe"
the Boche in his new positions.
Two 6" Martins were soon placed in
positions off "Newport trench" and
a 9.45" was got into action in
Surrey ravine. An ideal
spot for it. La Vacquerie was
the chief target. Some good
shooting was observed on the
sunken road which lead to
Marcoing. During the last
few days we were there we had
about 45 casualties from gas.
On the 22nd we were relieved by
the 36th Divisional Trench Mortars
The rest of the Division had

at Nesle by train. We then marched to Voyennes where fairly good billets were found. The Officers of the Brigade at this time were Acting D.T.H.O. Capt Grant

"X" Battery | "Y" Battery
Lt. Vincent | Capt Neill
2/Lt. Ayam | 2/Lt Smith
2/Lt. Perkins | 2/Lt Argyle
 | 2/Lt Hayes.

Capt Glen left the Brigade on 31st January. At about that time the Heavy Battery was made Corps Troops and the three medium batteries were formed into two — "X" & "Y" Batteries. All R.G.A. men were sent away with the Heavy Battery.

Most of the time at Voyennes was spent in training.

At midnight on the 21st March orders were received to proceed at once to Villers St Christophe. We had been there a few hours when more instructions came in to reconnoitre R.T.M. positions in front of Villers St Christophe and to find positions to cover the bridges over the Somme from Ham to St Simon. This was done but as there was no ammunition available and the infantry were withdrawing from in front of Villers St Christophe the Brigade moved back to already been relieved and were marching north.

We entrained independantly at Ytres and arrived at Ebblinghem on the 26th. Next day moving next to Renninghem. A very happy 8 days were spent here. The inhabitants were most hospitable people and did all they could to make the men more comfortable. Lorries took us to Jans Cappel near Bailleul. Another pleasant two weeks were spent there until we relieved the 19th Division in the Gheluvelt sector. A more difficult country for Trench Warfare would be hard to imagine. The country was nothing but flooded shell holes and it was impossible to dig a foot down in that season. One heavy position was taken over on the edge of Inverness Copse and a me defense position on the Menin Road about 400 yards from Gheluvelt. Not very much firing could be done here, as the ammunition supply was so difficult. Pill boxes at "Lewis" House and Gheluvelt Chateau were used mostly.

When we were relieved by the 17th Division two more offensive and 6 defensive positions had been built.

A few days were spent at Unbecque and at 5 am on the 25th February the Brigade arrived

OVER

Ham. Instructions were then received to retire to Esmery Hallon. No lorries could be obtained so all stores had to be destroyed and abandoned to enable the guns to be got away on the few G.S. wagons we had as transport.

After some difficulty we managed to get in touch with R.A. Head Quarters again and we were ordered to attach ourselves to Corps Hd. Quarters at Roye. We moved with them from Roye to Moreuil and from Moreuil to Oresmaux finally joining the 92nd Brigade R.F.A. at Jerancourt. A few days were spent there and then we marched to Villers Au Flaveuil close to Abbeville.

On the 18th April orders were received to move up to the line. The same morning we marched to Bettincourt and next day moved on to Rivery, a suburb of Amiens. We relieved the 58th Div T.M's on this front but as they had withdrawn all their guns it was necessary to find new positions. Positions were found a thousand yards or so in front of Villers Brettenaux but before work was commenced the Germans attacked and took the village. Villers Brettenaux was retaken the same evening next night.

On the evening of the 23rd orders came to have two

Beer a/c.

Date		£cs	Date			£cs
1919 Jan 4	To 100 ltr barrel stout	145	1919 Jan 4	Sales	Cash	15
			5	"	Cash	14
			6	"	Cash	11.40
			7	"	Cash	6.80
			8	"	Cash	6 -
			9	"	Cash	4
			10	"	Cash	14
			11	"	Cash	2
			11	Distribution	Cash	71.80
		£cs 145			Cash £cs	145

```
    145
     71 . 80
   ────────
     73   20
```

13.

two guns in the village by the next afternoon. Carrying parties and material were arranged for and 4 pm next day the guns were in position with 200 rounds beside them. There was not much difficulty experienced as the Boche did not shell the village heavily enough to prevent our carrying party of 100 men to get through the village three & four times without casualties. Three enormous vats of white wine only 30 yards from the guns were rather tempting to the workers. The two hundred rounds were fired that night on the Monument. Our only casualties were suffered then. The Boche putting a heavy barrage down on the village. The 4th Australians relieved us on the 28th and the detachments had a long walk down to Pont de Metz where we joined our transport.

Two days were spent here to clean up and the march to Lens was commenced. We spent a night at Bermenil, Wavans-Beauvois and Aounus finally arriving at La Targette where we took over our own line. The relief of the 5th Canadian Div. T.bty was completed on the 3rd of May. "Y" Battery took over positions in the Lens Sector. "X" Battery &

guns were in Saskatoon road
and in Avion. The positions were
about the best we had ever taken
over. The D.T.M.O's Head Quarter's
were in Givenchy this was
moved later to Rollencourt
on the Lieven Road.
On the 14th May Capt. Horther
joined the Division as D.T.M.O.
All the guns on this front were
connected to their Battery Head
Quarters by phone. A great advantage
which we had never had before.
The German Trench Mortars on this
front were rather active especially
in the Avion sector. They had
a good many positions behind
the railway embankment east
of Avion. Trench Mortar duels
would take place nearly every
afternoon. When we got to know
the front we could generally manage
to silence them. As soon as the
Germans T.M.'s started firing
their position was located by the
smoke of their discharge and
a couple of our trench mortars
would be turned on them
immediately.
In the Lens sector very successful
shoots were had on the Enemy's
line to assist our raiding parties
Raids were held frequently on
the whole of the Divisional Front.
One of our most uncommon jobs
was firing in the raid barrages

The German counter barrage was usually fell in the neighbourhood of our positions.

Up to the middle of August we were wholly on the defensive so work was continually being done on reserve positions almost as far back as Vimy ridge. A hundred rounds had to be carried to all these positions.

All Ammunition was brought up to within a mile of the actual positions by light railway and when the line was not broken the bombs were pushed up from there on trucks almost to the actual gun pits. Difficult enough but very easy compared with our former experiences of Ammunition supply.

We did not always have things our own way on this front, and it was not uncommon to have a position blown in.

Observation was usually done from behind walls of ruined houses in the outskirts of Lens and in Avion.

About the beginning of October the Germans started their withdrawal and an examination was made of his front line wire and T.M. positions. Very little wire was found intact and all his T.M. positions showed signs of damage, many of them having been completely destroyed.

On Oct 5th a gun was moved forward to a railway cutting on the southern edge of Sailfaumins. On the last night here two of our veteran N.C.O.s were killed. Casualties were not heavy on this front. One Officer was wounded. The casualties amongst the men were caused mainly from Gas and shelling.

Over 20000 rounds were fired while we where in this Sector. The Brigade was relieved by the 50th Div. Trench Mortars on Oct 6th and withdrew to the wagon line. Three days were spent at Maroeuil and on the 9th we moved forward to Chérisy with the Divisional Artillery.

Three weeks here were spent in training. The Brigade then moved up to Cambrai. ~~to take~~ On Nov 1st the Field Batteries moved forward to take part in the battle. As the Brigade had no mobile equipment all the men were attached to Field Batteries. On the day of the armistice our Head Quarters were in Bellignies near Bavay.

In such a small unit discipline was necessarily rather lax but this was made up by the excellent feeling between officers & men and the splendid esprit de corps throughout the unit.

CONFIDENTIAL

Vol 172

WAR DAIRY

20th Divisional Artillery Trench Mortar Brigade.

24.5.16 to 30.6.16

7.4.14

Army Form C. 2118.

WAR DIARY
or
INTELLIGENCE SUMMARY.
(Erase heading not required.)

20th Divl Artillery Trench Mortar Bde.
Date: 30th Nov - Dec 6th 1915/16 Mortar Brigade

Place	Date	Hour	Summary of Events and Information	Remarks and references to Appendices
Map Reference - Sheet 2B				
In the field on 24.5. 20 Divn. Front 2 vry C.22. central to I.11.d.10.0	24.11.5 20.11		Operation report :- X/20 Battery fired five rounds at Argyle Farm from C.28.t.7.7. (1 Gun) Result :- Very Satisfactory, 4 olive hits made, 1 blind.	WPG?
"	30.5 11		Operation report :- Y/20 Battery fired eight rounds at the Crater (S.11.d.9.2.h.) from Railway Wood. (1 Gun.) Result :- Very Satisfactory.	SSG
"	30.5 11		Operation report :- Y/20 Battery fired Seventeen rounds at Sap Head (S.12.a.4.2.) from Railway Wood. (1 Gun.) Result :- Unsatisfactory, owing to the Gun having to be forced to its full traverse the gun came over backwards & there was damage. Very considerable damage was done to enemy trench on the left of the objective.	SSG
"	2.6 11		Operation report :- Y/20 Battery fired Six rounds at Crater (S.11 & 9.2.h.) from Railway Wood. Result :- Very Satisfactory	SSG

Army Form C. 2118.

WAR DIARY
INTELLIGENCE SUMMARY.
(Erase heading not required.)

2.0" Div Arty Trench Mortar Brigade

Place	Date	Hour	Summary of Events and Information	Remarks and references to Appendices
Field	3/6		Operation report :- Y/20 Battery fired forty-nine rounds at Bat trench (J.12.a.4.2) from Railway wood. Result :- Satisfactory. A great # of direct hits made. Y/20 Battery fired one round at Crater (J.11.B.9.t.4) Result :- Satisfactory.	
Field	5/6	3-0 pm 3-10 pm	Operation report :- X/20 Battery fired seven rounds at The Mound (registration) from J.S.a.6.1. Result :- Satisfactory. 2 direct hits, 1 Blind.	
"	6/6	5-50 pm	Operation report :- Z/20 Battery fired 15 rounds at The Mound from S.S.a.6.1 at request from Left Group H.Qr Result :- Several direct hits made, 2 large breeches made in Parapet, also much damage done.	

Army Form C. 2118.

WAR DIARY
or
INTELLIGENCE SUMMARY.
(Erase heading not required.)

2nd Div. Arty. Trench Mortar Brigade

Place	Date	Hour	Summary of Events and Information	Remarks and references to Appendices
Field	4/6	9.30pm	Operation report:— Y/20 B battery fired four rounds at Enemy parapet (9.12.a.4.4.) from "Railway Wood" at request of Infantry. Result:— Satisfactory	Sgd/
"	7/6		Operation report:— Y/20 Battery fired eight rounds at 9.12.a.04. from Railway Wood. Result:— Satisfactory.	Sgd/
"	8/6	4·30pm & 6·50pm	Operation report:— Y/20 Battery fired twenty-five rounds at Enemy Salient from Railway Wood. Very considerable damage done. Result:— Satisfactory.	Sgd/
"	12/6	8·30pm	Operation report:— Y/20 Battery fired 2 Tons at Enemy Salient. (9.12.a.0.4) from Railway Wood at request of Infantry. Result:— Satisfactory.	Sgd/
"	13/6	12·30am	Operation Report:— Y/20 Battery fired nine rounds at Enemy Salient (9.12.a.0.4.) from Railway Wood. Enemy exploded mine opposite Railway Wood. Result:— Satisfactory.	Sgd/

Army Form C. 2118.

WAR DIARY
or
INTELLIGENCE SUMMARY.
(Erase heading not required.)

Instructions regarding War Diaries and Intelligence Summaries are contained in F. S. Regs., Part II. and the Staff Manual respectively. Title pages will be prepared in manuscript.

Army Troops Artly 2nd Div Motor Bde

Place	Date	Hour	Summary of Events and Information	Remarks and references to Appendices
Field	12/10	5–6 pm	Operation report :— V/20 Battery fired 14 rounds at Enemy Wire at the Salient (J.12.a.0.4.) for registration, from Railway Wood. Result :— Very Satisfactory	init
"	12/10	4·30 pm	Operation report :— X/20 Battery fired seven rounds at Enemy Wire at the Salient from (J.5.a.6.1.) Result :— Satisfactory.	init
"	13/10	1·30 pm	Operation report :— V/20 Battery fired 21 Rds. at the Enemys wire in front of Belleewaarde Farm. & also fired 16 Rds. South of Salient in front of Railway Wood. Result :— No report is obtainable as the Infantry did not go over at these points.	init
"	13/10	"	Operation report :— V/20 Battery fired 14 rounds. at Apex of Salient in front of Railway Wood. Result :— Very Good.	init
"	13/10	"	Operation report :— X/20 Battery fired 60 Rds at Enemy Wire at the Salient. Result :— Not Observed.	

Army Form C. 2118.

WAR DIARY
INTELLIGENCE SUMMARY.
(Erase heading not required.)

20th Div Arty Trench Mortar Batteries

Place	Date	Hour	Summary of Events and Information	Remarks and references to Appendices
Field	13/6/16	1·30 a.m.	Operation report :— Z/20 Battery fired 39 rounds at C. 29. a. 6. & 5. from S. 8. Result :— Not observed.	
"	16/6/16	7·3½ p.m.	Operation report :— V/20 Battery fired 1 round at suspected enemy Trench Mortar, from Railway Wood. Result :—	
"	17/6/16	12·30 a.m.	Operation report :— V/20 Battery fired 5 rounds at T.12.a.2.4. from Railway Wood, in retaliation. Result :—	
"	"	2·0 a.m.	Operation report :— V/20 Battery fired 5 rounds at I.12.a.2.4. from Railway Wood, in retaliation. Result :—	
"	"	9·10 p.m.	Operation report :— V/20 Battery fired 2 rounds at S.12.a.4.0. from Railway Wood, in retaliation. Result :—	

WAR DIARY

INTELLIGENCE SUMMARY.

Army Form C. 2118.

30th Div Arty Trench Mortar Bayset

Place	Date	Hour	Summary of Events and Information	Remarks and references to Appendices
Field	4/6/16	9.0 a.m	Operation report:- X/20 Bty fired 16 rounds, all D.A fuzes. Enemy wire from C 29 a 6.6. to C 29 A 11.	Enemy wire
"		10.0 a.m	Result:- Several Direct hits, effect excellent. Operation report:- X/20 Bty fired 20 rounds, S A fuzes. C 29 a 5.4. from C 29 c 8.1.	at Enemy wire
"		11.0 a.m	Result:- Several blinds, but result good, & wire breached. Operation report:- X/20 Bty fired 20 rounds, (D.A fuzes) at Enemy wire 9.5 6.5.4 from 9.5.0 a 6.1.	
"		11.15 a.m	Result:- Wire very much tormented about, (Ammunition suffered return in by enemy fire) Operation report:- V/28 Bty fired 24 rounds at Old Wire, SA face of Salient, 9, 1, a 0.4. Result:- Wire breached in two places.	

Army Form C. 2118.

WAR DIARY
INTELLIGENCE SUMMARY.
(Erase heading not required.)

Instructions regarding War Diaries and Intelligence Summaries are contained in F. S. Regs., Part II. and the Staff Manual respectively. Title pages will be prepared in manuscript.

20th Dir Arty Intell Notes 18 [?]

Place	Date	Hour	Summary of Events and Information	Remarks and references to Appendices
Field.	24-6-16	12.25p	1/20 fired 11 rounds at two Wire S. face of Salient S.12.a.0.4. from Poly Wood. Result was very satisfactory & wire badly damaged. Two Officers were slightly wounded during Operations.	Operation Orders
"	"	2-14p	1/20 fired 5 rounds on Wire N face of Salient from Poly Wood. Result satisfactory wire breached.	
"	25 to 26	9.0am 11.30am	2/20 fired 51 rounds at Wire S face of Salient at C.29 Central in two places & 16 yds in length.	
"	"	9.0 11.30 am	X/20 fired 60 rounds at Wire S. face of Salient at C.29 Central from S. of Lear Street. Result being very satisfactory. One Officer was wounded during operations, also 5 men. & 3 men were killed by enemy shelling, a direct hit being made on Gun Pit. 2nd Lieut D. A. Inge found to be unsatisfactory, causing many blinds.	

T2134. Wt. W708—776. 500000. 4/15. Sir J. C. & S.

WAR DIARY
or
INTELLIGENCE SUMMARY.

(Erase heading not required.) 20th Div Arty Trench Mortar Brigade

Army Form C. 2118.

Place	Date	Hour	Summary of Events and Information	Remarks and references to Appendices
Zuta.	25/7 to 10/10/15	10.15 am	X/20 fired 23 rounds at Wire & face of Salient C.29 Central from B of I Col B Red. result being satisfactory.	Operation Orders.
"	10/10/15		Z/20 fired 29 rounds at Enfilade trench B. face of Salient from S.8. result very satisfactory.	
"	"	2.30 pm	V/20 fired 11 rounds at S face of Salient from Rly Wood in retaliation for enemy shelling. result was very successful	
"	27/10/16	9.45	Y/20 fired 20 rounds at Enemy Wire C.29.D.5.4 from C.29 c.8.1. Result was very good.	
"	"	11.0 am	Y/20 fired 20 rounds at Enemy Wire S.5.b.54 from S.5 a 6.1 Result Good.	
"	"	11.15 am	V/20 fired 26 rounds at Wire & Salient 0.4 from Rly Wood. Result was very satisfactory	
"	26/10/16	5.6 pm	V/20 fired 19 rounds at Sap head from Rly Wood. Several D wire hits were made, but Sap Face was not damaged.	

Army Form C. 2118.

WAR DIARY
or
INTELLIGENCE SUMMARY.
(Erase heading not required.)

20th Div Arty Trench Mortar Brigade

Place	Date	Hour	Summary of Events and Information	Remarks and references to Appendices
Field	29/7/16	10 am / 5 pm	V/20 fired 5 rounds at Wire N.of Salient O.4. from Bly Wood. All rounds were effective & satisfactory	Operation Orders
"	"	"	V/20 fired 20 rounds at Wire B./n.e of Slain from Rly Wood. Very satisfactory result.	
"	"	"	V/20 fired 20 rounds at Salient O.4. from Railway Wood. Owing to weather conditions it was impossible to see extent of damage done	
"	"	"	V/20 fired 24 rounds at Enemy Wire A.12 to 6.7 from Muddy Lane. Wire was knocked in 3 or 4 places.	
"	"	12 m	V/20 fired 20 rounds at Salient O.4. from Railway Wood.	
"	"	"	" fired 3 rounds at transpt at A.8.12 to O.4. from Muddy Lane	
"	1/7/16	2-30 pm	Z/20. fired 2 rounds at L.R.B. Cottage from John Street. for registration. Results very good.	

M S Buckly
Capt RFA
O.C. T.M.O. 20th Division

20th Divisional Artillery

Trench Mortar Brigade.

J U L Y

(27.7.16 - 31.7.16)

1 9 1 6

Army Form C. 2118.

Trench Mortars

WAR DIARY
or
INTELLIGENCE SUMMARY

(Erase heading not required.)

20th DIVL. ARTILLERY TRENCH MORTAR BDE.
No. ....
Date 1.6.2.16

Place	Date	Hour	Summary of Events and Information	Remarks and references to Appendices
Zill.	7/6	3pm–5pm	Enemy shelled YPRES heavily with 5-9's but no damage done, firing mostly shrapnel.	Appx.
"	8/6	9 a.m.	Enemy shelled YPRES at a slow rate of fire for 2 hours.	Appx.
"	"	3 p.m.	Enemy again shelled YPRES for an hour with shrapnel.	
"	"	11-30 a.m	X/20 Battery fired 25 rounds at the Mound, which was badly knocked about & the result was entirely satisfactory.	Appx. (Group Operation Order)
"	9/6	10-0 a.m	Enemy shelled YPRES with 5-9's & 4-2'. but no damage done. Enemy aeroplanes were very active in & around YPRES.	Appx.
"	10/6	6 p.m.	V/20 Battery fired 5 rounds, at Enemy Trench Mortar at request of Infantry. enemy ceased fire immediately.	Appx.
"	"	10-32 pm	Y/20 Battery fired 9 rounds from Irmchurch Street at Enemy Wire (C.29.a.4.6)	Appx.

WAR DIARY
or
INTELLIGENCE SUMMARY

(Erase heading not required.)

Army Form C. 2118.

23th DIVL. ARTILLERY TRENCH MORTAR BDE.
No. ....
Date 3.0...7..1.6

Place	Date	Hour	Summary of Events and Information	Remarks and references to Appendices
Field			Result was not known owing to weather conditions.	Operation Orders
"	10/7/16	10.32pm	Z/20 Battery fired 20 rounds at the ground. Actual result was not known owing to dark.	M.S.S.
"	"	10.32pm	X/20 Battery fired 20 rounds from @ 39 c 8.2 at the ground. Result of firing was not known.	M.S.S.
"	11/7/16		The day passed very quietly, very few shells being fired.	M.S.S.
"	14/7/16	2.30am	V/20 Battery fired 21 rounds in retaliation for enemy trench mortaring. Enemy fire ceased.	M.S.S.
"	15/7/16	11.30	Enemy shelled YPRES very heavily to with 5-9"s a very light shelled for about 3 hours continuous, but no damage done.	M.S.S.
"	16/7/16	12.0pm	Relieved by 6th Divn Arty Trench Mortars less X/20 & Y/20 Batteries	M.S.S.
"	17/7/16		which were taken over by 6th Divn temporarily until 27/6	M.S.S.

Army Form C. 2118.

31

WAR DIARY
or
INTELLIGENCE SUMMARY
(Erase heading not required.)

H.S.Buckley
Capt B.G.O.
D.T.M.O. 20th Division.

20th Divisional Artillery.

20th DIVISION

TRENCH MORTAR BRIGADE

AUGUST 1 9 1 6

Vol 8.

CONFIDENTIAL
WAR DIARY
of
201st Div Arty
Trench Mortars
August 1916
VOLUME VI

Transfer from Artillery of 20th Div. to Arty. attached 24th Div.

WAR DIARY or INTELLIGENCE SUMMARY

20th DIVL. ARTILLERY TRENCH MORTAR BDE.

Place	Date	Hour	Summary of Events and Information	Remarks and references to Appendices
YPRES (in & out of July)	30-7-16	Midnight	Relieved the 6th Div. Arty. Trench Mortar Bde. on Left + Right Bde Trenches, night very quiet + relief was carried out in good order + no casualties. Z/20 By. went into Left Bde front + Y/20 By. into Right Bde front.	
	31-7-16		Everywhere in & around YPRES very quiet, work being done in erecting + strengthening dugouts + ammunition recesses on look out, also building gun emplacement.	
August	1 to 5-8-16			
	6-8-16		Enemy shelled YPRES with 4-2". not caualties.	
	7-8-16, 10:30am		Squadron of about 30 English Aeroplanes crossed over enemy lines, although heavily shelled by hostile Anti aircraft guns.	
	8-8-16	3-0 pm	YPRES Observation Balloons were observed from the Z. vicinity in the morning + again in the evening + at about 11-0 pm the enemy sent Gas over. The Stinkers Horns etc. gave good warning + Helmets were worn in mask helpful masks + no casualties occurred. Diurefine being maintained to mask casualties.	
	9-8-16			

Army Form C. 2118.

20th DIVL. ARTILLERY TRENCH MORTAR BDE.
No............
Date............

WAR DIARY
or
INTELLIGENCE SUMMARY.
(Erase heading not required.)

Instructions regarding War Diaries and Intelligence Summaries are contained in F. S. Regs., Part II. and the Staff Manual respectively. Title pages will be prepared in manuscript.

Place	Date	Hour	Summary of Events and Information	Remarks and references to Appendices
Zillo	9-4-16		Main Bde. Gas Helmets were renewed at 12-20 am	
"	10/5/16	10.0am	Our Artillery retaliated in splendid style. Enemy shelled YPRES heavily rate 4-2, & 5-9 + continued all day at a slow rate from 12-Noon, but no casualties received in the Bde.	
"	11/5/16	4 Nm	Enemy shelled the sanctuary for about 15 minutes with a high shell but none in damage 0 casualties were about	
"	12/5/16		Very quiet along the whole front.	
"	13/5/16	10 am	Enemy aeroplane crossed over YPRES and was at once engaged by our anti-aircraft guns. It retired when apparently unhurt flying at a very high altitude.	
"	14/5/16	11 pm	A very bright moonlight night. Hostile aeroplane flying low crossed our line as far as YPRES and dropped several bombs and returned immediately. We would ascertain no damage	
"	15/5/16	9 pm	Enemy Artillery bombarded YPRES with a few light shells which	

T2134. Wt. W708—776. 500000. 4/15. Sir J. C. & S.

WAR DIARY or INTELLIGENCE SUMMARY.

(Erase heading not required.)

Army Form C. 2118.

20th DIVL ARTILLERY TRENCH MORTAR BDE.

Instructions regarding War Diaries and Intelligence Summaries are contained in F. S. Regs., Part II. and the Staff Manual respectively. Title pages will be prepared in manuscript.

Place	Date	Hour	Summary of Events and Information	Remarks and references to Appendices
	16/8/16	2.30 am	did no harm. Hostile aeroplane again flew over YPRES, the night being favourable for night flying. Dropping bombs on the POTIJZE Road he dropped two bombs on a working party, which however went wide of the mark	
	17/8/16	3.30 am	Strong horns gave warning of approaching gas which did not arrive at YPRES on account of the wind springing up in another direction. The men were instantly aroused and smoke-helmets were donned	
		4.30 am	The signal having been given that there was no longer an immediate danger of gas, smoke-helmets were taken off and the men retired in an orderly manner. During the whole period of gas-alarm our artillery opened out to which the enemy offered no retaliation	
		6.30 pm	A few shells were dropped in the vicinity of the foundry but no casualties accrued	
	18/9/16	8 pm	Enemy shelled batteries in vicinity of foundry but	

Army Form C. 2118.

20th DIVL. ARTILLERY
TRENCH MORTAR BDE.
No............
Date............

WAR DIARY
or
INTELLIGENCE SUMMARY.
(Erase heading not required.)

Instructions regarding War Diaries and Intelligence Summaries are contained in F. S. Regs., Part II. and the Staff Manual respectively. Title pages will be prepared in manuscript.

Place	Date	Hour	Summary of Events and Information	Remarks and references to Appendices
	19/5/16	1 am	ceased on our artillery retaliating.	
		4.30 am	Enemy dropped one shell into the foundry at YPRES. Enemy dropped heavy shell into foundry. On neither occasion was any damage done.	
		3 pm	Enemy anti-aircraft gun engaged British aeroplane flying over foundry but failed to hit it.	
	20/5/16			

WAR DIARY
INTELLIGENCE SUMMARY
(Erase heading not required.)

Army Form C. 2118.

Place	Date	Hour	Summary of Events and Information	Remarks and references to Appendices
Field	26 Aug		Nothing to report.	
"	27/8-30/8		"	
"	30/8.	1.30 a.m.	3 rds fired on Mauser Bell Salient in retaliation to hostile T.M. fire.	
"	31/8.	5. a.m.	14 rds fired to silence enemy machine gun. Shooter John Stick. Result satisfactory but impossible to say if a direct hit was obtained.	
		10. a.m.	1 rd fired on Salient O.4. Rly Wood retaliation. Hostile T.M. ceased fire.	
"	1st Sept		Three Right Bole Front fired 32 rds according to O.O. result unobserved.	
			12 rds fired on Salient O.4 in retaliation Hostile T.M. fire. Result satisfactory. One premature, which wounded Capt Cockayne. Details not yet ascertained.	
			Three Left Bole front fired 32 rds according to O.O. These were fired in error owing to cancellation of orders not being received by M Scott in time.	

C.F. Roualle. Capt R.F.A.
4o X.T.M.O.

20th Divisional Artillery.

20th DIVISION

TRENCH MORTAR BRIGADE

SEPTEMBER 1 9 1 6

Confidential

War Diary of the

20th Div Arty Trench Mortar Brigade

1st September 1916.
to
30 Sept 1916

Army Form C. 2118.

WAR DIARY
or
INTELLIGENCE SUMMARY.
(Erase heading not required.)

Instructions regarding War Diaries and Intelligence Summaries are contained in F.S. Regs., Part II. and the Staff Manual respectively. Title pages will be prepared in manuscript.

Place	Date	Hour	Summary of Events and Information	Remarks and references to Appendices
Field	1/9/16		YPRES shelled evidently meant for Batteries. Aeroplane activity fair. Heavily shelled from both sides.	A818
	2/9/16		Aeroplanes all day fairly active.	
		7.30 P.M	YPRES heavily shelled. Shells appeared to be directed on the entrance, probably meant for convoys.	A818
		11.30pm	YPRES shelled apparently over Square 8 Prison.	
		11 pm	GAS ALARMS sounded. These were repeated at intervals of about 2 hours until about 3 am 3/9/16. Field Batteries responded in true style on hearing Gas alarm.	
	3/9/16	9-10	Aeroplanes (British) very active. They were shelled very heavily.	A818
		1.15pm	Germans put over two shells over near Dead end of Canal.	
		2.35	Three hostile planes (British) came over from enemy's lines being shelled until they passed over YPRES.	
	4-9-16	11am	Remainder of day very quiet round YPRES. British Aeroplane flew very low over YPRES.	A818

T2134. Wt. W708—776. 500000. 4/15. Sir J. C. & S.

Army Form C. 2118.

WAR DIARY
or
INTELLIGENCE SUMMARY.
(Erase heading not required.)

Instructions regarding War Diaries and Intelligence Summaries are contained in F.S. Regs., Part II. and the Staff Manual respectively. Title pages will be prepared in manuscript.

Place	Date	Hour	Summary of Events and Information	Remarks and references to Appendices
Field	4/9/16	1.30pm	Aeroplane passed over YPRES being shelled by enemy	1/888
		2.15pm	Enemy fired a few shells over YPRES	
		7pm	Enemy at intervals putting heavy shells over YPRES in direction of asylum.	
	5/9/16	9am	Guns behind foundry firing. One premature but no damage done to personnel.	2/888
		4.45p	Enemy commenced putting heavy shells over YPRES in direction of asylum.	
		6.30p	Enemy still putting occasional heavy shells over YPRES in direction of asylum. Remainder of night enemy very quiet.	
	6/9/16	1pm	A few aeroplanes flying about. British & enemy aeroplane had a battle in which enemy aeroplane was brought down. Other aeroplanes heavily shelled.	1/888
		2.15	Relieved by 4 Divl Arty Trench Mortar Bde.	

Army Form C. 2118.

WAR DIARY
or
INTELLIGENCE SUMMARY.
(Erase heading not required.)

Instructions regarding War Diaries and Intelligence Summaries are contained in F. S. Regs., Part II. and the Staff Manual respectively. Title pages will be prepared in manuscript.

Place	Date	Hour	Summary of Events and Information	Remarks and references to Appendices
Field	7/6	4 pm	About 2 pm Bde moved from Hardelogue to Base Details	A18/S
"	8/6	10 am	Bde entrained at Pont-Remy, + convoy proceeded by road, with the R.A.C.	A18/S
			Bde arrived at Calais about 6 pm + remained there until next morning.	
	9/6		Started again + reached Abbeville, + then on to Rouen - remained there for the night.	A18/S
	10/6		Started again + reached Hericourt nr Ribemont, + stayed in billets for 4 days.	A18/S
	14/6		Moved again to Bois De Tailles, + remained there until 30/6 when we proceeded to Meaulte Rd nr Fair toeing	
			Whilst staying at Bois De Tailles — X/20, Y/20 + Z/20 Batteries were sent to different field Batteries in the Division	A18/S
			Several night Hostile aircraft visited the camp vicinity	

T2134. Wt. W708—776. 500000. 4/15. Sir J. C. & S.

& drafted troubles but no damage was done to this Brigade.

J.M.McCarthy
Capt R.F.A.
O.R.M.O 20th Division

20th Divisional Artillery.

20th DIVISION

TRENCH MORTAR BRIGADE

OCTOBER 1 9 1 6

CONFIDENTIAL 10

Vol I

WAR DIARY

for

OCTOBER 1916

Trench Mortars
20th Division Artillery

WAR DIARY
INTELLIGENCE SUMMARY.
(Erase heading not required.)

Army Form C. 2118.

Instructions regarding War Diaries and Intelligence Summaries are contained in F. S. Regs., Part II. and the Staff Manual respectively. Title pages will be prepared in manuscript.

Place	Date	Hour	Summary of Events and Information	Remarks and references to Appendices
Field	1/10/16	11 am	Hostile aircraft dropped bombs near the camp, most of which failed to explode.	HqrS.
	2. 10/16		Nothing occurred of any great importance except Heavy enemy continually bombarding the enemy's territory.	HqrS.
	3. 10/16		There were 9 casualties to our men, which were attached to R.J.A.B batteries, a shell bursting amongst them, however luckily most were slight wounds.	HqrS.
	4. 10/16			HqrS.
	5. 10/16		Several men were attached to 10. A.C. + Y.d. Section + 1 Officer + 10. N.C.O. + 2 m went for a course in Heavy Trench Mortars, otherwise nothing of importance to comment on.	HqrS.
	to 10/16			HqrS
	20. 10/16		The weather on the average was fine.	
	21/10/16		2/Lt. H.J.S. Kendall. V20 Btty was invalided sick to England. 2/Lt. A. Munro-Ghon rejoined from England after recovering from wounds received in action in YPRES.	HqrS.
	25. 10/16		2/Lt. W.D. Armstrong 1/20 + Gnr. Tuttall 2. X/20 were killed in action + Lieut A. D. W. Sergt. X/20 was severely wounded + succumbed	HqrS.

WAR DIARY
or
INTELLIGENCE SUMMARY.
(Erase heading not required.)

Army Form C. 2118.

Place	Date	Hour	Summary of Events and Information	Remarks and references to Appendices
	26.10.16		to his magasadi on 26.10.16 The funeral of 2/Lieut. W. Donnachey and Lieut. W. Antrell, 2 Scots Guards at 11=0 am in Carnoy Cemetery. rain falling heavily during preceding & about 50 Officers + other ranks 9.Y.M.9. were present at the funeral.	AfS / ff.s.
	27/10/16 to 31/10/16		Nothing of much importance occurred. rain falling continuously.	

Jysauchly
Capt BZa.
9 Y.M.9. 20th Division.

20th Divisional Artillery.

20th DIVISION

TRENCH MORTAR BRIGADE

NOVEMBER 1 9 1 6

Vol XI

WAR DIARY
FOR
NOV 1st to 30th 1916

20th Divl. Artillery

TRENCH MORTARS

WAR DIARY or INTELLIGENCE SUMMARY

Army Form C. 2118.

(Erase heading not required.)

Instructions regarding War Diaries and Intelligence Summaries are contained in F. S. Regs., Part II. and the Staff Manual respectively. Title pages will be prepared in manuscript.

20th DIVL. ARTILLERY TRENCH MORTAR CDE.
Date 29-11-16

Place	Date	Hour	Summary of Events and Information	Remarks and references to Appendices
Build	1.11.16	—	Enemy aeroplanes were very active during the day & also dropped a few Bombs at night. Majority were some of which failed to explode, & very little damage was done.	
	"		The men in this Bde have been instructed but during the month 3 R.F.A Batteries etc. several have been constructed where been occupied. The weather has been very wet & cold, but the men have been made comfortable. We were reinforced with 10 men from D.A.C. on 6.11.16 & again with 6 on 25.11.16.	
	30.11.16		Capt. E.H. Small 1/20 was taken away to Hainin sick about 15-11-16 were not in action The Batteries 2" & 9.45" so there is nothing more of any importance to state. 2 Officers, M	

Army Form C. 2118.

WAR DIARY
or
INTELLIGENCE SUMMARY.
(Erase heading not required.)

Instructions regarding War Diaries and Intelligence Summaries are contained in F. S. Regs., Part II. and the Staff Manual respectively. Title pages will be prepared in manuscript.

Place	Date	Hour	Summary of Events and Information	Remarks and references to Appendices
			A.E.C. Dagwen I sent R.D.A. of D.M.O. 2nd Division	

20th Divisional Artillery

))))))))))))

20th /5 DIVISION

TRENCH MORTAR BRIGADE

DECEMBER 1 9 1 6

Vol 2

R. A. Trench Mortars.
20th Division

War Diary
December 1916

WAR DIARY or INTELLIGENCE SUMMARY

Army Form C. 2118.

Place	Date	Hour	Summary of Events and Information	Remarks and references to Appendices
Field	1-12-16 to 2-12-16		Personnel of all Batteries on Fatigue work for Field Batteries including crew of Hut, cleaning up Wagon lines & Salving horses of F.A. Brigade which had gone to rest Camps. R.E. Material supply to Batteries.	A/13
"	3-12-16		All men recalled from Fatigues except Hutting Parties.	A/14
"	4-12-16		Preparation for taking over line from 17" & 15 R.A.T.M.s.	A/14
"	5-12-16		Relieved 17" howitzers T.M.s in line	A/15
"	6-12-16 to " 24-12-16		During this period dug outs were erected to take 35 men, being 8 Island Avenue filling in it was impossible to continue on emplacements. Insufficient material was carried up to dug outs to Sunken Road West of Howard to complete two 2" emplacements. Ammunition chamber & dug outs to a depth of 20 feet. On morning of 24" handed over 16-17" Sies. R.A.T.W.s.	A/15
"	24-12-16		35 men attached to Left Group for Infirm	A/15
"	25-12-16		35 men attached to Right Group for Fatigues	A/15

Army Form C. 2118.

WAR DIARY
or
INTELLIGENCE SUMMARY
(Erase heading not required.)

Place	Date	Hour	Summary of Events and Information	Remarks and references to Appendices
field	27-12-16 to 31-12-16		The few men remaining in Camp employed on work in own Camp	Nil

H.B. Buckley
Capt. R.F.A.
Comdg. R.A. Trench Mortar Bde,
20th Division.

46/13

War
  Diary

R.A. Trench Mortars, 20th Division

Army Form C. 2118.

WAR DIARY
or
INTELLIGENCE SUMMARY

(Erase heading not required.)

Instructions regarding War Diaries and Intelligence Summaries are contained in F. S. Regs., Part II. and the Staff Manual respectively. Title Pages will be prepared in manuscript.

Place	Date	Hour	Summary of Events and Information	Remarks and references to Appendices
Field	1-1-17		Nil	Nil
"	2-1-17		2/20 personnel withdrawn from fatigue at Field Battery	App 1
"	3-1-17		2/- went into billets at Horlaimont for training	App 2
"	4-1-17		Nil	Nil
"	5-1-17		1/20 personnel withdrawn from fatigue at Batteries. Right Group fired to send down to men attached to them	App 3
"	6-1-17		Men attached to Right Group were sent down. (1/20)	
"	7-1-17		1/20 personnel proceeded to "Army T.M. School" on accordance with XIV Corps orders, to be there until 17th inst	App 4
"	8-1-17		Offs x r/s "went-over" Guards Div. front at another preparatory to taking over from them	App 5
"	10-1-17		X & Y Batteries proceeded to Combles to take over from Guards T.M.s. Firing 29: Six T.M.s also sent up to make the relief	App 6 App 7

Army Form C. 2118.

WAR DIARY
or
INTELLIGENCE SUMMARY
(Erase heading not required.)

Instructions regarding War Diaries and Intelligence Summaries are contained in F. S. Regs., Part II. and the Staff Manual respectively. Title Pages will be prepared in manuscript.

Place	Date	Hour	Summary of Events and Information	Remarks and references to Appendices
Field	12-1-17		"X" & "Y" Batteries withdrawn from Combles to Camp Trindles Pont.	AM
	16-1-17		2/20 returned to Camp Trindles Pont. X/20 went to Morlancourt	#740
	17-1-17		V/20 returned from Trench Mortar, & Army T.M. School	#741
	19-1-17		1/20 went and hellis at Combles to put in Heavy T.M. Emplacement	#743
	20-1-17		Y & Z Batteries also went and cut in lines & wheeled lines & "G's" T.M.S.	#1633
	20-1-17		Worked 4 to 6 in four 2" Emplacements. Also on one Heavy Position	AM
	22-1-17		on 22nd work stopped, & Orders Received to be "2" mining on the "9.45" Emplacement.	HF
			This was an idea of getting them on the only position on the front where a Heavy T.M. could be put in. Quickly as it the same time, have emplacement Flash cover and ammunition for the men and ammunition (Position being sniped at) very shortly trag	H831
	23-1-17		Work continued successfully on two emplacements which were prepared complete. Also two days work done on another Hvy position	#801
	27-1-17		Hindar over to 17" Division & returned to Trindles Pont	#891
	31-1-17		X/20 Proceeded to Franc to learn (4" Army T.M. School. Y/20 went to Morlancourt)	#712

H.H.M. McAfrey Capt A.A.
DTMO 20 X D.

2449 Wt. W1495/M90 750,000 1/16 J.B.C. & A. Forms/C.2118/12.

T M Sig gr
Vol 14

War Diary
of the

29th
DIVL. ARTILLERY
TRENCH MORTAR BDE.

WAR DIARY
or
INTELLIGENCE SUMMARY

(Erase heading not required.)

Army Form C. 2118.

Place	Date	Hour	Summary of Events and Information	Remarks and references to Appendices
Ald	8 Feb (Sun)		1/20 at 4"Army T.M. school. 1/20 at Redoubt. 1/20 + 2/20 at Minden Post. Training being done. 6. h. 8" 1/20 pract 4/20 rds 2" at practice. Grand very hard & bricks & like. D.A. fuzes acted excellently. 2 heavy guns sent away. 7	with headqrs. WDS
	10		1/20 + 1/20 returned to Minden Ron 1.	WDS
	11		4/20 rds fired from 29 "Dirian" –	WDS
	12 13 14		Reconnaissance made by Officers. Front line could not be approached except by night.	WDS
	16		Therefore in	
	18		1/20 + 2/20 recd orders to dig out at Ankles, ground very wet & dug out needed repair	
	19		2/20 commenced digging fork assurance of 5" R.E.s, for No. 2 emplacement. Found fire in pieces with orders to protect clay	WDS

WAR DIARY
or
INTELLIGENCE SUMMARY

Army Form C. 2118.

(Erase heading not required.)

Instructions regarding War Diaries and Intelligence Summaries are contained in F. S. Regs., Part II. and the Staff Manual respectively. Title Pages will be prepared in manuscript.

Place	Date	Hour	Summary of Events and Information	Remarks and references to Appendices
July	19		Attempts at digging in this place abandoned. Further reconnaissance made behind "Mercer Trench" ground very bad indeed.	ASS
	20			
	21		Further reconnaissance made by officers the ground found to be hopeless for T.M. emplacements & report to this effect made verbally to R.A. H.Qrs.	ASS
	22			
	23		Attempts made to reach "Mercer Trench" from Sunken Road, this three times of commencing digging. Party sniped shelled all the time.	ASS
	24		Further attempt made in m.28.c. 10th only a very few men. Two men wounded & party sniped & turned back.	ASS
	25		To work further.	ASS
	26		Relief made. D.m.B.T/20 going up the line.	ASS

Comdg. R.A., "... "
20th Division.

Confidential
Vol 75

"War Diary"

B.A. Trench Mortar Brigade
20th Division

March. 1917

Vol. 3

WAR DIARY
INTELLIGENCE SUMMARY
(Erase heading not required.)

Army Form C. 2118.

Place	Date	Hour	Summary of Events and Information	Remarks and references to Appendices
Field	8/2/17		X 20 Battery was relieved in line by Z 20	WBS
"	10/2/17		Y 20 Battery supplied 30 men as carrying party 2" trenches to new positions	WBS
"	11/2/17		Y 20 relieved Z 20 in line. Y 20 fired 11 rounds registration on wire. Bosnia salient from position of 509 support trench	WBS
"	14		Y 20 Battery was relieved by X 20	WBS
"	18		V 20 Battery sent 31 men to DAC for fatigues. 2/Lt Neild Y20 Bty attached to D92 Battery RFA	WBS
"	21		X 20 Battery came out of line	WBS
"	22		51 men sent from X, Y and Z Batteries to DAC for fatigues. Salvaging ammunition and cartridge cases left by field batteries at rear of gun positions in MORVAL area	WBS
"	23		2/Lt Grant and 2/Lt Murray attached to DAC for salvaging. Lt Barrat and a party of 20 men in charge of a general dump for DAC at BUS	HMS

WAR DIARY
or
INTELLIGENCE SUMMARY.

Army Form C. 2118.

Place	Date	Hour	Summary of Events and Information	Remarks and references to Appendices
Field	29/3/17		10 men sent to 4th Army Trench Mortar School Vaux-en-Amienois	SM8
			Inspected by Capt MA	
			DTMO 30" 5/S	

Confidential

Vol 16

WAR DIARY

R.A. Trench Mortars 20th Division

1st to 30th April 17

(Vol IV)

WAR DIARY
or
INTELLIGENCE SUMMARY.
(Erase heading not required.)

Army Form C. 2118.

Instructions regarding War Diaries and Intelligence Summaries are contained in F. S. Regs., Part II. and the Staff Manual respectively. Title pages will be prepared in manuscript.

Place	Date	Hour	Summary of Events and Information	Remarks and references to Appendices
Field	8.4.17		Brigade moved from CARNOY to COMBLES.	C.I.M.
"		2.0	Men of X/20 Bty were relieved from COMBLES dump	C.I.M.
"	10.4.17	2.0	Men of X + Y Batteries relieved Z/20 Bty from dump at BUS	C.I.M.
"	11.4.17		Captain Y. B. Berkeley R.F.A., M.C. attached to D/91. R.F.A. Bty.	C.I.M.
"	12.4.17	15	Men were relieved from COMBLES dump	C.I.M.
"	13.4.17	2/20	Party proceeded to 4th Army School of Mortars at VAUX-EN-AMIENOIS	C.I.M.
"	14.4.17	75	Bombs were salvaged from French Mortar Position in Bernia Salient	C.I.M.
"	15.4.17	14	Bombs were salvaged from Old French Mortar Position near MERCIA TRENCH.	C.I.M.
"				C.I.M.
"	17.4.17	11	men proceeded to dump on Bazenne Rd. also 2/lt R Murray R&R	C.I.M.
"	18.4.17	10	men x/20 + Y/20 returned from 4th Army School of Mortars at VAUX.	C.I.M.
EN-AMIENOIS				
"	16.4.17		Brigade moved from COMBLES to LECHELLES.	C.I.M.
"	21.4.17	2	Men from COMBLES + BUS dumps moved to NEUVILLE.	C.I.M.
"	23.4.17		5/0 Bty returned to LECHELLES from course at 4th Army School of Mortars	C.I.M.
VAUX-EN-AMIENOIS				

WAR DIARY
INTELLIGENCE SUMMARY.
(Erase heading not required.)

Army Form C. 2118.

Place	Date	Hour	Summary of Events and Information	Remarks and references to Appendices
Cuita	24/9/17		Lieut F.E.J. Dispucker R.F.A. 3/92 relieved 2/Lieut J. Mill R.F.A. from D/92 R.F.A. Battery.	C.V.S.A.
	26/9/17		2/Lieut J. Mill R.F.A. + one Aob proceded to 4th Army School of Musketry at NEUF-ENT AMIENOIS on 2" instructors course.	C.V.S.A. C.V.S.A.
	27/9/17			
	30/9/17		Work in camp etc.	

C.V.S. Mitchell Lieut R.F.A.
A.D.S.M.O. 20th Division

Vol 17

WAR DIARY
Trench Mortars 20th Division

1st May to 31st May 1917

Army Form C. 2118.

WAR DIARY
or
INTELLIGENCE SUMMARY.
(Erase heading not required.)

Instructions regarding War Diaries and Intelligence Summaries are contained in F. S. Regs., Part II. and the Staff Manual respectively. Title pages will be prepared in manuscript.

[Stamp: R.A. TRENCH MORTARS 20th DIVISION]

Place	Date	Hour	Summary of Events and Information	Remarks and references to Appendices.
Field	6.5.17	–	19 men attached to D/91. RFA in making Gun Positions &c	O.n.G
"	7.5.17	–	13 men were attached to 91st Bde RFA in making Gun Positions at 92nd	A.M.G
"	"	–		
"	8.5.17	–	2/Lt J. Neill RFA X/20 & L.T.M.G.O. returned from course at L.L school of Artillery 4th Army	A.M.G
			VAUX-EN-AMIENOIS	
"	9.5.17	–	Lieut R.V.S. Kitchens RFA X/20 attached to D/91. RFA	A.M.G
"	10.5.17	–	Lieut J.E.L Diesbecker X/20 returned from D/92 RFA	A.M.G
"	"	–	4 men X/20 19 Hy. Arty. not transferred to Howitzers & O.R.G Dump re petrol for threshing to School of Mortars.	A.M.G
"	11.5.17	–	Lieut K.G. Barrett. RFA Z/20 attached to Z/92 RFA	A.M.G
"	12.5.17	–	3/2/c. Battery appointed on T.M. Course – 2nd School of Mortars with Army. NYUX-ENAMIEWS	A.M.G
"	19.5.17	–	2/Lt L.S. Grant RFA Y/21 attached to Y/91. RFA	A.M.G
"	21.5.17	–	Lieut X. V. S. Hitching attached from D/91. RFA	A.M.G
"	20.5.17	–	2/Lt C.W Lt C.V.S Hitching RFA struck off strength on transferred to II Army School	A.M.G
"	"	–	of Artillery LIGNY.ST. FLOCHEL to undergo Trench Mortar course & to proceed to	A.M.G
			EGYPT, on termination of course.	
			all men attached to R.A. district & S.A.C Return to unit.	A.M.G

WAR DIARY
INTELLIGENCE SUMMARY

Army Form C. 2118.

Place	Date	Hour	Summary of Events and Information	Remarks and references to Appendices
FIELD	21.5.17	-	Advance party sent to new Camp near BERVIENCOURT and N°23 Cubel	Contd
"	22.5.17	-	2/LT. GARDOGGIN. RFA SR. 2/LT J. BLUNDELL R.F.A.S.R. 2/LT E.A. VINCENT, R.F.A S.R. joined from 31st Div. Arty.	Contd
"	"	-	reinforcements from 31st Div Arty.	Contd
"	24.5.17	-	2/LT. G.S. GRANT R.F.A. 2/20 rejoined unit from C/91 RFA	Contd
"	"	-	Y/20 R.M. returned from S. Athol. billets in VAUX-EN-AMIENOIS	Contd
"	25.5.17	-	CAPT. J.B. BUCKLEY, R.F.A.M.C. D.T.M.O. posted to 2/91 RFA	Contd
"	"	-	2/LT. (A/Captain) R. Munro. 9 L.N. RFA SR V/20 appointed D.T.M.O. vice Buckley.	Contd
"	"	-	HM Buckley Departed.	Contd
"	"	-	Recce Around for RECHULES to Camp near Beaulencourt and N°23 Central dy	Contd
"	"	-	Lewis on GS Waggons	Contd
"	26.5.17	-	Advance party Rnd off for new Camp near BEAUMETZ as in D.R.	Contd
"	27.5.17	-	All moved by Route . GS Waggons to H.Q.rs. BB. Wagons as sundry to	Contd
"	"	-	Wagon lines near BEADIEN COURT.	Contd
"	28.5.17	-	2/Lt's R.R.S. Atkinson and 2nd Burbridge Div. Amy T.M.B. in Ngsuil	Contd
"	"	-	took over ammunition from observation Dump	Contd
"	29.5.17	-	frames wag'n's moved on to HQ.r.	Contd

Army Form C. 2118.

WAR DIARY
or
INTELLIGENCE SUMMARY.
(Erase heading not required.)

Instructions regarding War Diaries and Intelligence Summaries are contained in F. S. Regs., Part II. and the Staff Manual respectively. Title pages will be prepared in manuscript.

Place	Date	Hour	Summary of Events and Information	Remarks and references to Appendices
Ytres	29.5.17	—	2/Lt E.J. McCarthy R.F.A. joined the B.d. as reinforcement from 2nd D.A.C.	Andf.
			Positions selected in the old Hindenburg line for 2, 2 inch emplacements & one Heavy, & Engineer assistance promised	Andf.
	30.5.17		Heavy mortar received from 4th Army Wksps.	Andf.
			Work started on 2 inch emplacements	Andf.

A Munro Elem Capt. R.F.A.
Comdg. R. A. Trench Mortars,
20th Division.

Vol 18

Confidential

WAR DIARY

20th Division Trench Mortars

1st — 30th June 1917

"War Diary"

Army Form C. 2118.

Instructions regarding War Diaries and Intelligence Summaries are contained in F. S. Regs., Part II. and the Staff Manual respectively. Title pages will be prepared in manuscript.

WAR DIARY
or
INTELLIGENCE SUMMARY.
(Erase heading not required.)

Place	Date	Hour	Summary of Events and Information	Remarks and references to Appendices
Field	1.6.17	4.30pm	Z/20 Bty relieved X/20 Bty in M² raid	A.C.I.
"	4.6.17	4 pm	Lieut. Dispatcho, 2/Lieut Blundell, & 2/Lieut Vincent, proceeded to 5th Army T.M. School at VALEREUX. on Y.M. course.	A.E.I.
"	5.6.17	6.30pm	Y/20 Bty relieved Z/20 Bty in line	A.E.I.
"			2 reinforcements joined from D.A.C.	A.E.I.
"	9.6.17	6.30pm	X/20 Bty relieved Y/20 Bty in line.	A.E.I.
"	12.6.17	5.30pm	Retaliation fire by medium & heavy mortars.	A.E.I.
"	13.6.17		Z/20 Bty relieved X/20 Bty in line.	A.E.I.
"	16.6.17	4.30pm	Medium fired into enemy wire.	A.E.I.
"	17.6.17	2 pm	Y/20 Bty relieved Z/20 Bty in line, and fired on enemy wire and mortar.	A.E.I.
"	20.6.17	11 am	Y/20 Bty fired on enemy wire & enemy mortar, & while firing enemy mortar opened fire but was at once engaged & ceased fire.	A.E.I.
"	20.6.17	9.30pm	Batteries relieved from line by 10 a/ M Bn	A.E.I.
"	28.6.17 to 30.6.17		Brigade moved to GUARNY, by lorrie. 9.5 began personnel worked Batteries taken in Gun Drill Rifle Drill Signalling & General Training	A.E.I.

A E Wiccgett Capt. R.F.A.
Comdg. R²L T/rench Mortars,
20th Division.

Confidential

Vol 19

War Diary

20th - 31st
1st - Div. Trench Mortars
1st
to 31st July 1917
9 (vol 3)

Army Form C. 2118.

20th Trench Mortars

WAR DIARY
INTELLIGENCE SUMMARY.
(Erase heading not required.)

Instructions regarding War Diaries and Intelligence Summaries are contained in F. S. Regs., Part II. and the Staff Manual respectively. Title pages will be prepared in manuscript.

[Stamp: R.A. TRENCH MORTAR No. 7011/2/704 Date 31-7-17 20th DIVISION]

Place	Date	Hour	Summary of Events and Information	Remarks and references to Appendices
Field	3-7-17	—	Brigade moved to ENGLEBELMER by lorries	A.M.9
"	4-7-17	—	" " " BARTON Area "	A.M.9
"	5-7-17	—	" " " REBREUVE "	A.M.9
"	6-7-17	—	Lyktook Div Arty + came to POPERINGHE AREA and ran to report to 116th Inf Bde. Batteries posted to Brents attached to 28th Divisin Trench Mortars as follows: X/20 + Y/20 to Left Grenh. Z/20 to Right Grenh. + V/20 to Heavy Grenh. 20th D.T.M.O. took command of Left Grenh	A.M.9
"	7-7-17	—	Line Reconnoitred	A.M.9
"	8-7-17	—	Batteries went into line, as no accomodation was available in Trenches	A.M.9
"	9-7-17 to 14-7-17	—	Batteries lined in Copse W. of Canal. Work on emplacements carried on. Ammunition carried up nightly.	A.M.9
"	12-7-17	—	day during this period	C.M.9
"			Lt F.C.K. Whitaker R.F.A. wounded (Gas) 2/Lt R.H.E. Murray R.F.A. assumed command of Y/20. This Battery now moved nearer by casualties, was retired from work in emplacements by V/81. V/20 token to her work of getting up ammunition.	G.M.9
"	13-7-17	—		A.M.9

2353 Wt. W2544/1454 700,000 5/15 D. D. & L. A.D.S.S./Forms/C. 2118.

WAR DIARY
or
INTELLIGENCE SUMMARY.
(Erase heading not required.)

Army Form C. 2118.

Place	Date	Hour	Summary of Events and Information	Remarks and references to Appendices
Field	15-7-17	-	Bombardment commenced. LT. K.G. BARRETT R.F.A. Z/20 was wounded. 2/LT. E. Vincent R.F.A. Z/20 took on temporary command of Z/20.	Am.9
"	19-7-17	-	Z/20 transferred to left flank.	Am.9
"	21-7-17	-	LT. J.E.L. D. Waterton R.F.A. returned from Hospital.	Am.9
"	22-7-17		Y/20. Detachment of Y/20 relieved.	Am.9
"	24-7-17		2/LT. 19. A. Coggins R.F.A. Y/20 wounded. (Gas)	Am.9
"	25-7-17		Y/20 Take over from Y/38 who withdraw from the line	Am.9
"	30-7-17		T.M'S amalgamated. This Bombardment & batteries were withdrawn to Rear Billets. LT. K.G. Barrett R.F.A. returned from Hospital & resumed command of Z/20.	Am.9
"	31-7-17		Y/20 Proceed to line, in poor day ahead, the regiment during the advance, 30 men proceeded to line to act as stretcher bearers.	Am.9
"			T.M'S Bombardment of front line mud & trench were very effective. Trench & wire being obliterated within a few days of commencement of Bombardment.	Am.9

F. Munro Ellen
Comdg. R.A. Trench Mortars,
Capt. R.F.A.
20th Division.

Brigade Orders by Captain A. M. Glen R.F.A.
D.T.M.O. 20th Division

Wednesday 1.8.17

Reports etc

B.C. will render a return of deficiencies in stores & equipment as early as possible.

Inspection

A Kit inspection of reinforcements who have joined Battery since going in the line on 8th inst. should be made by B.C. & any deficiencies reported immediately to this Office.

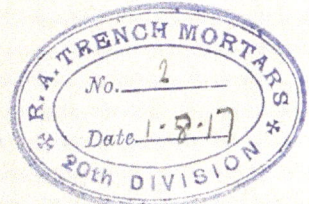

A. Munro Glen Capt. R.F.A.
Comdg. R. A. Trench Mortars,
20th Division.

CONFIDENTIAL.

WAR DIARY

R.A. TRENCH MORTARS 20TH DIVN.

1ST – 31ST AUGUST, 1917.

WAR DIARY
INTELLIGENCE SUMMARY.
(Erase heading not required.)

Army Form C. 2118.

Place	Date	Hour	Summary of Events and Information	Remarks and references to Appendices
Field	1.8.17		40 men proceeded to line + attached to R.A, M.T. etc	A.m.g.
"	3.8.17		2/Lt R.H.C. Murray R.F.A V/20 admitted to Hospital (Wounded Gas)	A.m.g.
"	"		2/Lt J.B. Lindall D.F.A 2/20 went in A are now camp Boulogne for a fortnight	A.m.g
"	4.8.17		2/Lt F. Fisher-Smith R.F.A. joined Brigade + posted to Y/20 TMB	A.m.g
"	5.8.17		19 Reinforcements joined from sch of D.A.C.	A.m.g
"			4 un uniformed from sch. all classes strong be shown	A.m.g
"	8.8.17		To be moved to barracks camp near Proven for rest + training	A.m.g
"	9.8.17 to 19.8.17		D.A.C. turned Transport Training proceeded with in Batteries + Ball signalling classes with R.F.A. V/20	A.m.g
"			2nd Lt. C.J. M. Carthy R.F.A. appointed (a/Captain) and	
"	12.8.17		3/Lt (A/Adjut) F.G.H. D Lapscha R.F.a. appointed S.T.M.O.	A.m.g
"			Captain A.S. Jones 9/Lin R.F.A. appointed 2 i/c command X/20 T.M.B	A.m.g
"			2/Lt G.S. Evans R.F.A. appointed (a/Lt) to command 2/20 "	A.m.g
"			2/Lt R.F. D. Welch R.F.A. appointed (a/Lt)	A.m.g

Army Form C. 2118.

WAR DIARY
or
INTELLIGENCE SUMMARY.
(Erase heading not required.)

Place	Date	Hour	Summary of Events and Information	Remarks and references to Appendices
Field	15.5.17		Reinforcements joined D.A.C. from 20th D.A.C.	Amly
"	16.5.17		2/Lt. Lyall RFA was appointed A/Lt. & Command 2/1st T.M.B.	
"	"		Captain a Munro Glen R.F.A. & 2/Lt. G.S. Grant M.C. proceeded on leave to England	Amly
"	18.5.17		Returned to S.H.B. camp.	
"	19.5.17		60 men were attached to D.A.C. as ammunition fatigue. 2/Lt. Q.L. Colonel LT Eyall accompanied party who [illeg] returned to camp on 21.5.17	Amly
"	"		2/Lt. C.J. McCarthy R.F.A. + 2/Lt. F. Hellier-Smith R.F.A. + 25 men proceeded to 5th Army T.M. School	Amly
"	"		2/Lt. G.E. Vincent 2/20 attached to 2/1/2 R.F.A.	Amly
"	10.5.17		General fatigue in camp, Gun Cleaning, Stores etc	Amly
"	23.5.17		"	
"	24.5.17			
"	30.5.17		Lt. I. Audel R.F.A. proceeded on leave to England	Amly
"	31.5.17		2/Lt. I. McDonnell & was attached to D.A.C. on Gun fatigue. returned to camp	Amly

G. Munro Glen Capt. R.F.A.
Comdg. R. A. Trench Mortars, 20th Division.

CONFIDENTIAL

Vol 21

War Diary

of

20th Divnl. Arty. Trench Mortars.

From: 1.9.17.

To: 30.9.17.

Volume 9.

CONFIDENTIAL

(6202) W 11186/M1151 350,000 12/16 McA. & W., Ltd. (Est. 781) Forms/W 3091/3. Army Form W. 3091.

Cover for Documents.

Nature of Enclosures.

WAR DIARY

Notes, or Letters written.

Army Form C. 2118.

WAR DIARY
or
INTELLIGENCE SUMMARY.
(Erase heading not required.)

Instructions regarding War Diaries and Intelligence Summaries are contained in F. S. Regs., Part II. and the Staff Manual respectively. Title pages will be prepared in manuscript.

Place	Date	Hour	Summary of Events and Information	Remarks and references to Appendices
Field	4.9.17	—	2/Lt. A. W. Y. Incani R.F.A. Z/22. T.M.B. Struck off strength (Wounded) whilst attached to D/92. R.F.A.	Appx
"	6.9.17	—	2/Lt. J. Burrell R.F.A. X/20. T.M.B. Transferred to D/92. R.F.A.	Appx
"	7.9.17	—	Lt. G. S. Grant R.F.A. M.C. X/20, 2/Lt. G. A. Coggin R.F.A. Y/20 + 2.Lt Mann Appointed to 8th Army T.M. School at Valheureux. Took over H.446" T.M. + 3. 6" Newton T.M. from 39th Divnl. Trench Mortars.	Appx
"	8.9.17	—	Took over from Siege camp 15 camp near Ziedenbrugh. S.A.A. Ammunition Transport.	Appx
"	"	—	Relieved 58th Divn. Trench Mortars, who had one 6" in action in Langemark. Wagm limber Ammn. Shelled, dy enemy 6 lnei. men killed.	Appx
"	12.9.17	—	Fired 171 Rds. 6" on cement dugouts on Eagle trench + on wire.	Appx
"	17.9.17	—	Completed work on second Emplacement + brought second 6" into action.	Appx
"	18.9.17	—	Fired 197 Rds. 6" firing both mortars, on Eagle trench Cemetery + strong points.	Appx
"	20.9.17	—	Lt. K.G. Barritt. R.F.A. &R. Z/20. killed in action + 12 men killed + wounded	Appx

2353 Wt. W2544/1454 700.000 5/15 D. D. & L. A.D.S.S.;Forms/C-2118.

Army Form C. 2118.

WAR DIARY
or
INTELLIGENCE SUMMARY.
(Erase heading not required.)

Instructions regarding War Diaries and Intelligence Summaries are contained in F.S. Regs., Part II. and the Staff Manual respectively. Title pages will be prepared in manuscript.

Place	Date	Hour	Summary of Events and Information	Remarks and references to Appendices
Field	23.9.17		2 N.C.Os. + 10 O.Rs. attached to 59th Bde. Only for building winter dug-out lines etc.	Amm
"	24.9.17		1 N.C.O. + 10 O.Rs. attached to 61st. Ask for building number N.C.Os + men. Same also also men from 92nd Bde.	Amm
"	25.9.17		Officers + men returned from T.M. School.	Amm
"	26.9.17		7 plaque patrols of 35 men. Artillery. Parties composed of men acting from the line.	Amm
			Fired 40 Rounds. 6" on O. Good to Western Farm under very heavy enemy fire.	Amm
"	27.9.17		Fired 67 " 6" on same target. Exploded two dumps	Amm
"	28.9.17		Fired 25 " 6" strong points	Amm
"	29.9.17		Fired 20 " 6" strong points.	Amm
"	30.9.17		Went round positions + pointed out targets to O.T.M.O. + officer of 4th Div. Trench Mortars, preparatory to handing over to them.	Amm

G. Munro Glen Capt. R.F.A.
**Comdg. R. A. Trench Mortars,
20th Division.**

CONFIDENTIAL.

WAR DIARY.

OF

20TH. DIVNL. ARTY. TRENCH MORTARS.

From 1st October to 31st. October. 1917.

VOL. 10.

Army Form C. 2118.

WAR DIARY
or
INTELLIGENCE SUMMARY.
(Erase heading not required.)

Instructions regarding War Diaries and Intelligence Summaries are contained in F. S. Regs., Part II. and the Staff Manual respectively. Title pages will be prepared in manuscript.

[Stamp: N° TRENCH MORTARS, R.A., No., Date, 20th DIVISION]

Place	Date	Hour	Summary of Events and Information	Remarks and references to Appendices
Field	1.10.17	1 pm	Relieved by H.T. Divisional T.M's. Batteries returned to march area	V.E.C.O.
"	2.10.17 to 10.10.17		ELVEDINGHE. Cleaning guns. Equipment. Signalling & marching drill.	V.E.C.D.
"	3.10.17		Captain ;a minor 9 Gun R.T.A. proceeded to X/06 Army T.M. school in England	O.T.E.C.O. O.T.E.C.O.
"	8.10.17		2/Lt. A.E. Vincent sy minor unit from sick leave	
"	11.10.17		Capt. A 9 minor 9 Gun R.T.A. returned from X/06 Army T.M. School	V.E.C.D.
"	12.10.17		2/Lt. J. Johns Smith R.H.A. returned to unit from Hospital	
"	14.10.17 to 16.10.17		6 Officers & 70 O.R. attached to 83 Bde; daily for screening Guns Position & repairing camouflage at Batteries	V.E.C.O.
"	16.10.17		2/Lt E.J. McLaulchey proceeded on leave to England	V.E.C.O.
"	19.10.17		2/Lt. A.E. Vincent R.T.A. 2/20 to command Z/20 (vice Lt. H.G. Barrett R.T.A. "Killed in Action")	V.E.C.O.
"	20.10.17	4 pm	Relieved by 35th Divisional artillery Trench Mortars and came into Billets near ELVEDINGHE 1 Gun 6" & 9 Medi 6" bombed out by John Bale.	V.E.C.D.

Army Form C. 2118.

WAR DIARY
or
INTELLIGENCE SUMMARY.
(Erase heading not required.)

Instructions regarding War Diaries and Intelligence Summaries are contained in F. S. Regs., Part II. and the Staff Manual respectively. Title pages will be prepared in manuscript.

Place	Date	Hour	Summary of Events and Information	Remarks and references to Appendices
5 A	20.10.17	6 pm	Brigade moved by M.T. lorry from camp near ELVERDINGHE	V.E.CO.
"	21.10.17		PROVEN & PESELHOEK, detrained for the SOMME	V.E.CO.
"	22.10.17		Arrived at PERONNE & then proceeded to HEUDICOURT by lorry	V.E.CO.
"	23.10.17		Captain A. Munro Gen. R.F.A. proceeded on leave to England, Captain J.E.L. Disbrowe taking over Temporary Command of Brigade	V.E.CO.
"	24.10.17		Relieved 40th Divisional Artillery T.M. in turn	V.E.CO.
"	25.10.17		Received 7 casualties to Personnel of X/20 T.M.B.	V.E.CO.
"	26.10.17	11 am	Moved to camp near Fins, transport provided by D.A.C.	V.E.CO.
"	27.10.17		2/Lt. J.S. HOYLE R.F.A. Armee R.dc & posted to Z/20 T.M.B. also 18	V.E.CO.
"	27.10.17 28.10.17		reinforcements from D.A.C. 2/Lt. J.S. HOYLE R.F.A. 2/20 proceeded to "NEWTON" 6" T.M. School	V.E.CO.
"	28.10.17	6 P.M.	X/20 T.M.B. moved again to camp at HEUDICOURT. Transport furnished by D.A.C.	V.E.CO.
"	29.10.17		X/20 T.M.B. fired 16 rounds 6" NEWTON.	V.E.CO.
"			Y/20 " " 14 " " " "	
"			Z/20 " " 3 " 2" T.M. (Reg'd Baton)	V.E.CO.
"	30.10.17	6 am	Half of X/20 relieved remaining men of Y/20 in Line	V.E.CO.

V.E.L. Disbrowe Capt RFA

CONFIDENTIAL.

Vol 23

WAR DIARY.

OF

TRENCH MORTARS 20th Divl Arty

From 1st Nov'17 to 30th Nov'17

VOL. II

Reference Sheet 57c. Trench Mortars Army Form C. 2118.
1:40,000 20" Div Art

WAR DIARY
or
INTELLIGENCE SUMMARY.
(Erase heading not required.)

Instructions regarding War Diaries and Intelligence Summaries are contained in F.S. Regs., Part II. and the Staff Manual respectively. Title pages will be prepared in manuscript.

Place	Date	Hour	Summary of Events and Information	Remarks and references to Appendices
Field FINS	1.11.17		Fired 5 rds 2" on Enemy Wire.	Cundy
	2.11.17		Continued supply in carrying ammunition to forward area & material for constructing T.M. Emplacements in VILLERS PLOUICH & GONNELIEU	Cundy
	3.11.17		Fired 10 rds 2" & 12 rds 6" NEWTON on enemy M.G. & T.M. Position.	Cundy
	4.		Infantry & R.E. working Parties temporarily attached for carrying timber & ammunition & Sapping for T.M. Position.	Cundy
	5.11.17		"	Cundy
	6.11.17		Fired 22 rds 6" NEWTON & 5 rds 9.45" at Enemy wire (X Reg'stering) Wear after being opened up on morning of 22 " no reply. Enemy Trenches & Wire.	Cundy
	7.11.17		" 10 " 9.45" T.M. 6.17 " " 9.45	Cundy
	8.11.17		" 2 " 6" " in retaliation.	Cundy
	9.11.17		" 25 " 6" at Enemy Wire & T.M. emplacements.	Cundy
			Enemy retaliated with Heavy T.M. whilst firing	Cundy
			Capt. J.E.K. DIESPECKER R.F.A. admitted to Hospital (Sick). 2/Lt B.A. Coggins takes over temporary command of V/20.	Cundy
	10.11.17		Fired 40 rds 6" NEWTON & 5 rds 9.45" on enemy wire... good result.	Cundy
			Wire obtained to ga/s during run in wire.	Cundy

Army Form C. 2118.

WAR DIARY
or
INTELLIGENCE SUMMARY.
(Erase heading not required.)

Instructions regarding War Diaries and Intelligence Summaries are contained in F. S. Regs., Part II. and the Staff Manual respectively. Title pages will be prepared in manuscript.

[Stamp: TRENCH MORTARS 20th DIVISION]

Place	Date	Hour	Summary of Events and Information	Remarks and references to Appendices
Gilla.	11.11.17	.	Fired 10 rds 6" NEWTON at enemy wire	amy
"	12.11.17	.	Fired 93 rds 6" " " 6 rds 9.45" in short range concentration	amy
"	13.11.17	.	Fired 8 Mor " 6 rds 9.45" at enemy Trench	amy
"	14.11.17	.	Fired 22 rds 6" in short range concentration.	amy
"	15.11.17	.	Fired 5 rds 6" at enemy wire	amy
"	16.11.17	.	Handed over to 12th Dy T.M.B. 404 rds 6" NEWTON, 2nd Division joining amy	joining amy
"	18.11.17	.	2nd Fired 11 rds 9.45" in enemy Trench & concentration in GONNELIEU & T.M EMPLACEMENT	amy
"	19.11.17	.	D.T.M.O. moved from HEUDICOURT to VILLER PLOUICH.	amy
"	20.11.17	6.20am	In the attack of the Division our Mortars joined in covering barrage. 6" NEWTON firing 515 rds & 9.45" (Lng Russian) 22 rds On an average 3 c/s were mar by each mar during the attack. Target being mainly M.G. emplacements & T.M. firing & South were very satisfactory. No casualties occurred to mm Personnel during firing.	amy
"	"	"	Handed over to 40th Div. T.M. 102 rds 6" NEWTON & 36 rds 9.45"	amy

Army Form C. 2118.

WAR DIARY
or
INTELLIGENCE SUMMARY.

(Erase heading not required.)

Instructions regarding War Diaries and Intelligence Summaries are contained in F.S. Regs., Part II. and the Staff Manual respectively. Title pages will be prepared in manuscript.

[Stamp: R.A. TRENCH MORTARS — 20th DIVISION]

Place	Date	Hour	Summary of Events and Information	Remarks and references to Appendices
In field	21.11.17		Y/20 & X/20. Batteries got into action with enemy. Guns & fired 240 rds 7.7 mm & 516 rds 10.5 c.m. on enemy working parties.	Arty.
"	"		SERANVILLERS, LESDAIN, CREVECOEUR. Dumps of enemy working parties.	Arty.
"	23.11.17		Handed over to 29th Division T.M. 260 rds 6" NEWTON & 7 mortars (6" NEWTON) & Bdis	Arty.
"	24.11.17			Arty.
"	to		X 20. & Z 20 Batteries carried out work on salvage of guns & enemy Mortars & Guns. 14 guns being taken to Corps Salvage Park Gouzeaucourt	Arty.
"	"			Arty.
"	27.11.17		Handed over to 20th D.A.C. 2 Mortars & Beds (6" NEWTON)	Arty.
"	28.11.17		Batteries returned from line to VILLERS PLOUICH	Arty.
"	"		2.Lt. C.J. McCarthy R.F.A. Y/20 transferred to 92nd Bde R.F.A.	Arty.
"	"		1/Lt G.A. Coggin R.F.A. Y/20 proceeds on leave to England	Arty.
"	29.11.17		Officers & men of 29th Divl. T.M. returned their units	Arty.
"	"		Company reports on salvage of Mortars	Arty.

WAR DIARY
or
INTELLIGENCE SUMMARY.

(Erase heading not required.)

Army Form C. 2118.

Place	Date	Hour	Summary of Events and Information	Remarks and references to Appendices
Fins	30/11/17	9:15am	On enemy attack 10 anyone withdrew with 6" NEWTON Comy. to METZ & then to FINS	

A. Newton(?)
Comdg. R.A. T.M. ...
20th Division

Vol 24

WAR DIARY 20th Div. Trench Mortars

DECEMBER 1917

(Vol 12)

WAR DIARY / INTELLIGENCE SUMMARY

Army Form C. 2118.

Place	Date	Hour	Summary of Events and Information	Remarks and references to Appendices
Fula	1.12.17		Parties from X, Y, Z Batteries returned to their respective units	Cont.
"	2.12.17		Batteries worked on clearing stores & guns	Cont.
"	3.12.17		4 Officers were attached to 91st Brigade R.F.A.	Cont.
"	"		2/Lt M.S.G Lewis R.F.A. joined Bde & posted to 91st Bde R.F.A.	Cont.
"	4.12.17		2 Officers returned from being attached to 91st Bde R.F.A.	Cont.
"	5.12.17		40 men from Y/20 & X/20 were attached to 21st D.A.C. in Dunk.	Cont.
"	6.12.17		Reconnoitred for positions in front of La Vacquerie	Cont.
"	7.12.17		Y/20 & Z/20 went out to the line to prepare T.M. positions	Cont.
"	"		Battery personnel & M.G's from guns	Cont.
"	8.12.17		Continued work on T.M. emplacements	Cont.
"	9.12.17		40 men attached to D.A.C. returned to their units	Cont.
"	"		2/Lt F. Fisher, Smith RHA returned from attached 10/9 17 F.A.	Cont.
"	"		Continued work on T.M. positions	Cont.
"	10.12.17		Fired ammunition spray rounds 15 rds 6" Newton mortars extended	Cont.
"	11.12.17	9am	Fired 12 rds 6" Newton on registration on Zero line	Cont.
"	"	5pm		Cont.

WAR DIARY or INTELLIGENCE SUMMARY

Army Form C. 2118.

Place	Date	Hour	Summary of Events and Information	Remarks and references to Appendices
India	1/12/17		1/20 & 2/20 returned by 1/20 & 2/20 on the line. Moved an enemy	Army
"			Heavy T.M. employment returned.	Army
"	13/12/17		Bombarded on ammunition about on the Vas Querie firing 10 eds 6" Newton.	Army
"	"		2/Lt W.G.A Parker R.F.A returned from an attached 10/9/17 R.F.A	Army
"	13-15/12/17 12/N		Bombarded in conjunction shoots on the Vas Querie firing 12 eds 6" Newton.	Army
"	"	16.35/N	Our trench mortar from lines shoot to maintain on line till relieved by our T.M.B	Army
"	14.12.17		2/Lt W.G.A Parker R.F.A & 2/Lt O.P. Immediate R.F.A. to Army T.M. School at Vachennan	Army
"			on T.M. Course fired 5 eds 9.45" T.M. MK III on the Vas Querie	Army
"	15/12/17		fired 1 rd 9.45" T.M. MK III on enemy sap	Army
"	16/12/17		Tramlines moved to Baulue our & attached to H/21 Section 20th D.A.C	Army
"	17/12/17		2/Lt T. Helm-Smith R.F.A & Lt C.S. Grant R.F.A M.C. 1/6 O.R. wounded (Gas) admitted to Hospital	Army

WAR DIARY
or
INTELLIGENCE SUMMARY.
(Erase heading not required.)

Army Form C. 2118.

Place	Date	Hour	Summary of Events and Information	Remarks and references to Appendices
Fully	18.12.17	1 a.m.	G. an scramblers received to proceed. & consulted 61st Div	Amly
"	"		Early an to relief by them T.M.s, informer they would med to arrange	Amly
"	19		into the lines that our unit would be relieved by 36th Div T.M.	Amly
"	19.12.17		Went round T.M. positions with D.T.M.O. 36th D. Division preparatory to handing	Amly
			over to them	
"	20.12.17	11 Noon	7/100 V/60 were relieved in the line by 36th Div T.Ms	Amly
"	21.12.17		Lt G.E. Grant & 2/Lt H. Helen Smith returned from Hohai.	Amly
"	25.12.17		A.de entrained at YTRÈS Station. Transport was provided by 61st D.A.C	Amly
"	26.12.17		arrived at Hislingham Station no Transport available	Amly
"	27.12.17		Marched by lorries to Huvringham	Amly
"	30.12.17		2/Lt H. Helen Smith proceeded on leave to England	Amly
"	31.12.17		L/L Hogg Q.2a " " " "	Amly

A. Murrough Capt R.F.A.
Cmdg. R.A. Trench Mortars,
20th Division

CONFIDENTIAL.

WAR DIARY

OF

20th Div. Arty. Trench Mortars.

From 1st Jan 16 to 31 Jan 18

VOL. I.

WAR DIARY
INTELLIGENCE SUMMARY
(Erase heading not required.)

Army Form C. 2118.

Hour	Summary of Events and Information	Remarks and references to Appendices
1.1.18	Brigade Moved from HEURINGHAM. Lay Moton Lorries to ST. JANS CAPPEL	A. M. G.
	In rest. Training.	
9.1.18	T.M. Transfers rejoined unit from being attached 5 D. A. C.	G. M. G.
15.1.18	2/Lieut. G. S. Grant & Lt. J. Neill proceeded on leave to England	G. M. G.
20.1.18	2/Lt. S. G. Lewis & party returned from T.M. Course	G. M. G.
	& Lt. S. Hayes & 11 men proceeded to 2nd Army T.M. School	G. M. G.
	in general.	
21.1.18	Brigade moved from ST. JANS CAPPEL by Motor Lorries to Camp	A. M. G.
	Belgie Camp.	
	Relieved 37th Division T.M.s in the Line	
	Paid 20 ads 6d Newton on LEWIS HOUSES with satisfactory results.	G. M. G.
	15 " " "	G. M. G.
	10 " " "	G. M. G.
	10 " " "	G. M. G.

20th Division.

T. M. Bde.

February 1918.

WAR DIARY
or
INTELLIGENCE SUMMARY.

Army Form C. 2118.

20D TMB February 1918

Place	Date	Hour	Summary of Events and Information	Remarks and references to Appendices
Irish	4.2.18		Captain A. Munro G.S.M. R.F.A. D.S.M.O. transferred to 9th Argyll R.F.A. as Captain G.S. Munro R.F.A. M.C. taken over command	
"	"		2/Lt. K. Hyam R.F.A. joined Bde from 20th D.A.C.	
"	2.2.18		Command of 2/20 T.M.B. proceeded to 4th Army T.M. School at VAUX-EN-AMIENOIS on T.M. Course	
"	"		2/Lt. S. Hyam Q.F.A. & 2/20.T.M.B. proceeded to 2nd Army T.M. School. Handed over 12 Mortars to 6th Div. T.M., & received 10 6" NEWTON	
"	"		On reorganization scheme Bde was divided up. Personnel of Y/20 T.M.B. being transferred to 22nd Corps (H) T.M.B. X, Y & Z/20 Batteries formed (new) & a Y/20 Batteries.	
"	5.2.18		2/Lt. D.C. Douglas R.F.A. posted to Bde from D.A.C.	
"	6.2.18		2/Lt. G.A. Coggins R.F.A. Y/20 transferred to 22nd Corps (H) T.M.B.	
"	9.2.18		3 new 2" m/bs 6" Newton at ZHELUVELT wood	
"	9.2.18		Handed over 9.45" T.M. & Ammunition to x Lt. Corl. (H) T.M.B	
"	10.2.18		Fired 5 rds 6" Newton on Enemy M/gun m/fs position	
"	11.2.18		Fired 11 rds 6" Newton on Enemy H/mor	

Continued

WAR DIARY
or
INTELLIGENCE SUMMARY
(Erase heading not required.)

Army Form C. 2118.

Place	Date	Hour	Summary of Events and Information	Remarks and references to Appendices
Field	15.2.18		Fired 5 rds 6" Newton on Eclewelt Wood.	
"	17.2.18		Captain E.R. Grant proceeded to T.M. School.	
"	18.2.18		Brigade moves from Cafe Belge to St Jans Capel.	
"	19.2. "		Capt. E.S. Grant + 2/Lt H. Jones returned from T.M. Course.	
"	21.2.18		Brigade moves from St Jans Capel to Morbecque by Motor Lorries.	
"	24 " "		2/Lt Vincent + 3/1450 O.R.s + Party returned from T.M. School.	
"	28 " "		Entrained Steenbecque Station to Voyennes.	
"	" " "		Early " " H.Q + W.C.o. + Men. proceeded to Cresk. On special duties (Interpreters R.A.)	
"	" " "		Coy " " " Proceeded Cresk. Reporting at R.A.H.Q	

[signed] Capt. R.F.A.
O.C. 00° day R. A. Trench Mortars,
20th Division.

20th Divisional Artillery.

TRENCH MORTARS

20th DIVISION.

MARCH 1 9 1 8

Vol 27

CONFIDENTIAL.

WAR DIARY
of
R.A. Trench Mortars. 20th Divn.

From 1st to 31st March 1918

Vol III

(6339) Wt. W160/M3016 1,500,000 10/17 McA & W Ltd (E 1898) Forms W3091.　　　Army Form W.3091.

Cover for Documents.

Nature of Enclosures.

Notes, or Letters written.

Army Form C. 2118.

WAR DIARY
or
INTELLIGENCE SUMMARY.
(Erase heading not required.)

Instructions regarding War Diaries and Intelligence Summaries are contained in F. S. Regs., Part II. and the Staff Manual respectively. Title pages will be prepared in manuscript.

March.

Place	Date	Hour	Summary of Events and Information	Remarks and references to Appendices
Field	4/3/18		12 Men proceeded to Erchin and reported at R.O.H.Q.	
	7		2/Lt W.C.E. Perkins & 20 admitted to 66.I. thro sick	
	9		H.Q. Habt. & Men returned from Erchin	
	10		R.O.Q. Men returned from Erchin	
	12		2/Lt Hynn proceeded on leave to England	
	15		20 H.Q.O.R. Men proceeded for the purpose of rehearsing at the 30th Div A.C.	
			Order to stand to, ready to move at any moment	
	21		Orders to move at 11.45 a.m.	
	22		Moved from Yzeucourt at 2.15 a.m. (Motor lorries delayed) arrived at Villiers M Christophe	
			at Villiers we had to join about immediately, and proceeded to Engays Haller	
	23		Moved off from Engays Haller at 7.15. am and proceeded to Rosis	
	25		Moved off from Rosis at 1.2 pm and arrived at Morcuil 8.45.	
	26		Orders to Proceed too	
	27		Moved off from Morcuil at 11.15 pm and arrived Crusmcur at 4.30 am on 28.3.18.	
	2			

[signature] Lt. R.F.A.
Cmdg. R.A. French Mortars.
30th Division.

CONFIDENTIAL.

Vol 28

WAR DIARY.
of
20th R.A.T. Mortars
1st to 30th April 1918
Vol IV

WAR DIARY or INTELLIGENCE SUMMARY.

Army Form C. 2118.

April 1918

Place	Date	Hour	Summary of Events and Information	Remarks and references to Appendices
In the Field	2.4.18		2/Lt Hare evacuated into hospital	
	7.4.18		Moved from Gomiécourt to Achiet-le-Grand. T.M. Transport proceeded further in the day	
	17.		Moved to Lucheux	
	18.		Moved from Villers-au-Flos and Mareuil by T.M. Transport	
			Arrived at Villers-au-Flos and Mareuil and proceeded to Pierret, breaking the journey at Villeneuf	
			y Bolling planned to proceed to the line, this was cancelled later	
	20.		Battery proceeded to Busy to harness camp	
	22.		Groups of mules ready to ever position	
	23.		Two officers and 52 O.R. proceeded to Ammunition dump	
	27.		Battery proceeded to the line at Bussu Wood. Position on being finished is subject	
			Own detachment stayed and fired 130 rounds at Villeneuf and surrounding roads	
	28.		No. 1 of this detachment being wounded	
			Received one two-6" Newton gun from positions of the 4th Australian T.M. Brigade, the 2nd T.M. Batt.	
	29.		Moved off from Nature to Pierreuil, en route received two-6" Newton from T3 Aust from	
	30.		3rd Australian D.A.D.O	
			2/Lt L C Wynn rejoined	

Signed,
Capt. R.F.A.
Cmdg. R.A. Trench Mortars,
20th Division.

No. 29

CONFIDENTIAL

WAR DIARY
of
R.A. Trench Mortars, 20th Divn.

1st to 31st May 1918

Vol. V

(6339) Wt. W160/M3016 1,500,000 10/17 McA & W Ltd (E 1898) Forms W3091.   Army Form W.3091.

Cover for Documents.

Nature of Enclosures.

Notes, or Letters written.

WAR DIARY or INTELLIGENCE SUMMARY

Army Form C. 2118.

Month: May 1918

Place	Date	Hour	Summary of Events and Information	Remarks and references to Appendices
In the field	1st		Arrived from Beauval & proceeded to Beauvois. Repairs by Lorries. Brigade Horses from Beauvois to Houdain Al Jorques	A/M.P.
	2nd		Houdain to Sgt George H Lorries	A/M.S.
	3rd		Relieve 3rd Canadian Trench Mortar Brigade	A/M.P.
	4th		Fired 10 rounds in the neighborhood of Neufstering	A/M.P.
	5th		99 " on Enemy Machine Gun Trench Mortar Positions	A/M.P.
	6th		70 " on Enemy Trenches + New entanglements with good results. 1/20 taken over Left Section of the Line	A/M.P.
	7th		100 " Positions	A/M.P.
	8th		90 " Positions and good effect	A/M.P.
	9th		T M Brigade H.Q. moved from Ennevelin to Rollencourt. 75 rounds expended on Enemy Trench Mortar Positions	A/M.P.
	10th		100 rounds expended on T M + M G Positions	A/M.P.
	11th		75 " " Bivouacs and T M Positions	T/M.S.
	12th		Captain A.W. Heather Royal Berks Regt arrives to command 20th R.O. T M/B	A/M.P.
	13th		100 rounds fired on different Targets	A/M.P.
			50 rounds fired on Gun Groups + T M Positions	A/M.P.
	14th		Fired 31 rounds on Dugouts and T M Positions	A/M.P.
	15th		The Enemy TM were very active and several rounds dropped in Orion Trench. Four O.R. Douglas transferred to A/91 Bde R.F.A. expended 130 rounds on harassing fire	A/M.P.
	16th		Material harassing fire was kept up on Dugouts + Trenches Bridge. Several direct hits were	A/M.S.
	17th		Expended 171 rounds on different Targets. Beams destroyed — T M Positions hung the edges of Mise	A/M.P.
			Expended 110 rounds on Trenches	A/M.P.
	18th		Enemy artillery very active. The village of Orion appears. Fired 150 rounds on Beams destroyed Bridge Green Envoiers attacked	A/M.S.
			Left Section fired 90 of these. 6 NCO/men of 1/20 Brigade	A/M.P.
	19th		Fired 85 rounds on different Targets. Mobile T M actively on our front line. Normal	A/M.P.

WAR DIARY or INTELLIGENCE SUMMARY

Army Form C. 2118.

Month: **May 1918**

Place	Date	Hour	Summary of Events and Information	Remarks and references to Appendices
In the Field	20.		Fired 110 rounds on Green Grassier T.M. + M.G. Positions	4M.P.
	21.		" 157 " " Semi Destroyed Bridge Road around N8/C.2.4 tree	4M.P.
			Wire entanglements.	
	22.		Fired 105 rounds on different targets.	4M.P.
	23.		Fired 110 " on Green Grassier + T.M. positions followed by infantry	4M.P.
			Hostile T.M. fired a few rounds into Avion Village, but immediately silenced	
	24.		Fired 153 rounds. Observed shoot. 20 rounds on dugouts + trenches	4M.P.
			65 rounds on scattered targets dugouts Terraced + H.T.M. replacements.	
			T.Muscillance Shoot. J.C. Hayes reports the effect from 1st Army reinforcement camps	
	25.		Fired 105 rounds on following targets, dugouts, today T.M.G. Positions with good effect	4M.P.
			Telephone station awakement for 24 hours from May 26 to 6am 27 May 18.	
	26.		Fired 175 on different targets. The funeral passed the Village of Rollencourt by 4pm and TM	4M.P.
	27.		Fired 103 rounds on following targets T.M. + M.G. positions. 2 H.T.M. located at N27C99.50	4M.P.
	28.		Expended 107 on following 15 rounds on barrage, remainder on TM in support of infantry Raid	4M.P.
			Remainder of ordnance on different targets. H.T.M. materially answered on front	
	29.		245 rounds expended on targets. Seconds. H.T.M. Position living the Brigade Rear. mit	4M.P.
	30.		very good result, many direct hits obtained. Shelling on the left sector.	4M.P.
			Expended 83 rounds on Trenches, 12 rounds on dugouts 40 rounds on Trenches. M.G. Positions	
	31.		Remainder on observation on following targets. Were dugouts. Rounds 12 T.M. Positions	4M.P.
			Expended 142 rounds on following targets, dugouts, redoubts 12 T.M. force + other targets	

J. Heber Smith
4/4 A&SH Lt. Col. R.E.T.M.

Vol 30

CONFIDENTIAL

WAR DIARY
of
20th R.A. Trench Mortars
from 1st to 30th June 1918
Vol. VI.

(6392) Wt. W6192/P875 1,500,000 4/18 McA & W Ltd (E 2815) Forms W3091/4.   Army Form W.3091.

Cover for Documents.

Nature of Enclosures.

Notes, or Letters written.

Army Form C. 2118.

WAR DIARY
or
INTELLIGENCE SUMMARY.
(Erase heading not required.)

June 1917.

Instructions regarding War Diaries and Intelligence Summaries are contained in F.S. Regs., Part II. and the Staff Manual respectively. Title pages will be prepared in manuscript.

Place	Date	Hour	Summary of Events and Information	Remarks and references to Appendices
In the Field	1.6.17		Fired 91 rounds on different targets. Embankment dugouts & wire. Used German Grenade. Exploded. Enemy Replies nil. L.T.M. AVION.	
	2nd		Fired 137 rounds on various targets	
	3rd		173 " 28 rounds informed on embankment at A26.b.61.45. eight direct hits were obtained. 35 rounds observed on Enemy L.T.M. along Embankment from N.33.a.60.a0.16	
	4th		Fired 322 rounds. 2/Lt C.H. Pritchard proceeded to ENGLAND on Leave (Special) 212 rounds on different targets including CULVERT HTM FOSSE, direct hits well obtained. Rate on surface of MG N.33.d.12.82, N.33.b.05.10. Trench N.33.b.10.06. N.33.b.1f.25.	
	5th		Fired 107 Rounds on targets N14.a.6.5. N14.C.40.05. N14.C.35.36. slight Enemy Gas Shelling at 11.30 p.m. on positions N14.W.5. N14.C.40.45 N14.b.72.52	
	6th		" 222 " 58 rounds on HTM D N33.b.7.7. HTM M al 23+26 OP 59 NCT 20 rounds were fired	
	7th		Fired 248 rounds on positions D N20.a N14.C 36.25. D HTM D N20.C 85.30 + N20.C.8.5 also OPs on Green Grassier 20 rounds on assault HTM at N.33.a.8.9	
	8th		Fired 248 rounds on Assault N14.d 81.33 N 20.a. N.a. 99 N14 N4 67 Enemy Riddled with HTM + L.T.M. Telephone undermined from 7 a.m till 6 a.m 10 a.m	
	9th		Fired 218 rounds 7 rounds on Fosse D N.14.C. 20 round on TM 51 and other targets	
	10th		Fired 275 " 116. MG.12 Various Embankment D N 27.C.90.45. N33.a.62 4 TM 2) N.33.b.12. Enemy replies nil L.T.M. in AVION. 20 rounds on TM 12 6.3 at NT 65.22 on N33.6.18. + direct hits were obtained	
	11th		Fired 195 rounds on different targets	
	12th		Fired 236 " 30 rounds on TM 12 T.M.51 + T.M.55. 25 rounds on Sewer Exit at N.14.C.45.46. 30 rounds on T.M. at N.14.d. 81.33. 106 rounds and Bridges D N.26.6 4145 dugout N 27.C.90.00 HTM at N.27.C.86 25 More Silent dugout N.33.a.93.90. M T.M.22 direct hit were obtained	
	13th		Fired 160 rounds 25 Rounds on T.M.57 area Houses ruined N.20.a.20 Enemy TM 0.5cm and 7.7 MM Were active intermittently (TM on Green Grassier engaged 30 rounds landing in Fired 60 rounds 10 rounds at H.T.M in Cemetery Salient. 7 rounds on N14.C.45. 7 rounds on N14.C.H.-3	
	14th		15 rounds on N14.C. 00.50.	
	15th		Fired 60 rounds 30 rounds at H.T.M. in Cemetery + dugouts at N.33 a 85.95. 30 rounds on N.14. C.05-65 with good effect	
	16th		Fired 187 rounds 80 rounds on Werf of N.14.C.02.55 70 rounds on Crater at N.56. a.41. dugouts at N 33 a 93.80 HTM D Exploding 10 rounds on Fosse. Telephone Exchanged from 62 4th Jan 1914. A.E. Vincent, X'no proceeded on Gas Course. A. Arthur Capt

2353 Wt. W2544/1454 700,000 5/15 D.D.&L. A.B.S.S/Forms/C. 2118.

Army Form C. 2118.

WAR DIARY or INTELLIGENCE SUMMARY.

(Erase heading not required.)

Instructions regarding War Diaries and Intelligence Summaries are contained in F. S. Regs., Part II. and the Staff Manual respectively. Title pages will be prepared in manuscript.

Month: June 1918

Place	Date	Hour	Summary of Events and Information	Remarks and references to Appendices
In the Field	17th 1918		Fired 110 rounds 66 rounds on H.T.M. at N27.c.90.40 + H.T.M. at N33.a.9.9 more stores and 32 rounds on Wire at N14.c.1.1 wire cutting on Wire + Clog Trench	
	18th 19th		Fired 72 rounds on approved targets. Telephone suspended.	
			" 196 " 45 rounds on Wire at N14.C.67.60	
			HTMs at N27.c.90.40, N33.b.1.7 HTM 23 rounds on N14.c. 41.60.41 rounds on Mire	
	20th		Fired 56 rounds. 45 rounds on Wire N14.c.08.40. Enemy replied with Med Trench Mortars on AVION	
	21st		Fired 73 rounds on Series Ex+ Dugouts + HTMs	
	22nd		" 145 " on H.T.M. at N27.c.90.30. N33.a.95.90. Mr Cochran Posted from 204 Batt B 16 1/20 Battery. 1 NCO + 9 men attached from 204 C.A.B.	
	23rd		"Lieut VINCENT. A.E. received back from Gas Course.	
			98 rounds fired on H.T.Ms + dugouts N27.c.90.40 and N33.a.9.9. N34.c.72.57 and Fosse No 1	
	24th		Fired 160 rounds " various targets "	
	25th		Fired 12 " " " dugout H.T.M. L.T.M + M.G. emplacement	
	26th		" 81 " " on Targets HTM. at N33.a.19-8 "	
			" 110 " dugouts + H.T.M N27.B.30.25	
			N33.a.9.8. Also various night targets at N21.c.1-0. 20 Nights fired from M.D.H.	
	27th		Fired 81 rounds on dugouts HTM and MG N27.c.18.18, N27.c.99.50	
	28th		" 57 " on dugouts, HTM N27.c.90.30 and aft Ground N20.a N14.c	
	29th		Expended 143 rounds on L.T.M at N33.a 60.80 dugouts at N33.a M.T.M at N33+30.a N83+20.60 N27.c.90.30 20 rounds on N14.c 35.55. 15 rounds N14.c.H.2. 15 rounds on	
			N20.a H.E. Lieut. Kendall Baker from 3/88 A.F.B surgeon 1/20 T.M.By.	
	30th		Expended 124 rounds 109 rounds dugouts at N33.a 8.9. H.T.MS N27.c.9.4. 10 rounds Interdiction fire. 15 rounds on dugouts Mr Robertson Capt — 20th C.A.6. DTMO 20th Dn.	N14.c. 43.72. 1. VII. 1918

2353 Wt. W2544/1434 700,000 5/15 D. D. & L. A.D.S.S./Forms/C. 2118.

Confidential.   Vol 32

WAR DIARY.

of

20th T.M.A. TRENCH MORTARS.

From 1st to 31st July 1918

Vol VII.

(6392) Wt. W6192/P875 1,500,000 4/18 McA & W Ltd (E 2815) Forms W3091/4.   Army Form W.3091

Cover for Documents.

Nature of Enclosures.

Notes, or Letters written.

Army Form C. 2118.

WAR DIARY
or
INTELLIGENCE SUMMARY.
(Erase heading not required.)

July 1918

Place	Date	Hour	Summary of Events and Information	Remarks and references to Appendices
In Trenches	1.7.18		Expended 130 rounds on following targets 14 rounds on N20.a.4.8. 16 rounds on N14.c.1.7. 100 rounds on T.M.s at N33.b.00.80. N27.c.90.30. N33.a.90.80. N33.b.53.25. Hostile T.M. active.	
	2 "		Expended 97 rounds on targets 12 rounds on N.14.c.42.60. 85 rounds on H.T.M. at N33.a.9.8.	
	3 "		Expended 120 rounds on targets 31 rounds on N14.c.7.7. 82 N.27.c.94. N33.a.95.90. Hostile T.M. replied, 3 men 24/120 wounded (gassed)	
	4 "		Expended 173 rounds. 10 rounds registration shoot on N20.a.4.4.21 rds on N14.c.2.5. 80 rds on 6in H.T.M. + Dugouts at N.27.C.9.4.	
	5 "		Expended 160 rds. 20 rds on Force 1. 30 rds on N14.c.44. 20 rds fired on N14.c.0.5. Lieut. C.H. Pritchard reports back from England. Sergt Mann reports from being attached to large B.G. P.G.A.	
	6 "		Expended 160 rds. 70 rds on N20.c.6.7. miscellaneous targets H.M.s nunneries	
	7 "		Expended 136 rds on different targets.	
	8 "		Expended 209 rds. 30 rds on N20 Avre 2.60. 30 rds on N 20.C.9.F. 40rds on Force 1. N14.C.W.6. 89 rds H.T.M. L.T.M. Dugouts Force 5 at N.30.a.7.7. N33.b.5.2. N20.a.45.82. and N.27.c.99.50. 1 NCO + 2 Other Ranks passed to Rest Camp at Audrescelles.	
	9 "		Expended 103 rds. 73 rds fired on Dugouts at N 33.a.7.7. N33.a.1.7.n. 27.c.9.4 and Reserve T.M. N33 Central. 30 rds fired on N14.a.0.5.	
	10 "		Expended 210 rds. Bn Bns destroying and engaging this enemy N33.a.9.8. H.T.M. at N33-7-8. N.27-c-9-4. Force 5. 9 rds M.Gun Dugouts at N.20.a. + 3.67. Enemy Artillery roth active T.M.	

WAR DIARY or INTELLIGENCE SUMMARY

Army Form C. 2118.

Month: July

Place	Date	Hour	Summary of Events and Information	Remarks and references to Appendices
In the Field	11.7.18	—	Expended 126 rds 60 rds on H.T.M and Dugouts at N.33.a.9.8. 66 rds at N.20.a.45.80 and N.14.c.10.35.	
	12.7.18	—	Expended 195 yds 70 rds on Fosse 5. Dugouts at N.20.6.50.10. 30 rds on N.20.a.4.9. 6 rds on N.14.c.20. 19 rds on N.20.a.15. 3 rds on N.20.c.30.85. 17 rds on N.13.a.95.55. 20 rds on 20 rds on N.14 at 10. Capt. G.S. Grant N.C. & 20. T.M.B.Y. proceeded on Special Leave.	
	13.—	—	152 Expended. 27 rds on Troops at N.14.c.1.7. 100 rds on M.G. at N.33 a. 05.95. H.T.M. Lens Station Fosse 5. and Dugouts at N.20.a.45.35. 25 rds on wire at N.14.c.05.60 10 NCO & men posted from 22nd B&C. and 9th Bde R.F.A.	
	14.—	—	Expended 220 rds. 94 rds on Troops at N.20.a.8.2. 70 rds on H.T.M. & Dugouts at N.27.c.90.20 N.27.a.9.35. and N.33.a.92.53. Enemy T.M's Mollied with our own rds. 58 rds on Bridge N.20 a.5.95.	
	15.—	—	Expended 201 rds 26 rds on Bridge N.20a.20.95. 15 rds on Tunnel N.20 a 45.85. 10 rds on Wire at N.14.c.15.60. 17 rds on T.M's 100 rds on Lens Station Fosse 5. Dugouts L.T.M. – M.T.M's. at N.20.a.45.55. N.33.a.0.8. N.33 a. 92. 33. 15 rds on Obs.T. N.20.a. 33.95. 22 rds on Bridge N.20.a. 20.95.	
	16.—	—	Expended 166 rds. 81 rds on Lens Station Fosse 5. at N.20 a 45.55. 85 rds on Fosse N.20.c.49. anti Oom attack.	
	17.—	—	Expended 111 rds. 20 rds on Bridge at N.20.a.1.9. 11 rds on Wire N.14.c.05.60. 65 rds on H.T.M's, L.T.M's & Dugouts at N.33 a. 92.35. N.33.b.00.80. N.27.c.90.20. 2nd Lt. A.F. Vincent & 20 T.M.B.Y. posted to 9th Bde. R.F.A.	
	18.—	—	Expended 212 rds 20 rds on Fosse St Louis 16 rds N.20 a 3.6. 2 rds on T.M. N.20 a 95. Thro T.M 6 rds Reinf. of Bofors Mouflin. 105 rds wire on Fosse 5. Culvert at N.20.a. 62.40. 2nd Lt N.S. W.33.a. 00.30. and N.33.c.92.53. Lieut. W.V. Kendall & 20 Transferred to 4/20 T.M.B.Y	

Army Form C. 2118.

WAR DIARY
or
INTELLIGENCE SUMMARY.
(Erase heading not required.)

Instructions regarding War Diaries and Intelligence Summaries are contained in F. S. Regs., Part II. and the Staff Manual respectively. Title pages will be prepared in manuscript.

Month: July.

Place	Date	Hour	Summary of Events and Information	Remarks and references to Appendices
In the Field	19.7.15		Expended 160 rds. 60 rds on Dugouts at N27c.9-3. MG at N33a.05.98. LTMs at N33.b.00.88. This being a Balloon Shoot. 30 rds on N.1.C.2.5. 20 rds N20a.10.g.	
	20—		20 rds on N20a 49.30 rds on N20a 4.5.	
	21—		Expended 171 rds at different targets	
	22		Expended 200 rds on N.1.1.c.1.2. 20 rds N14c.88.25. 21 rds on N14.c.3.1. 100 rds on Fosse 5. LTM Duty. LTM at N33.f.00.86. N33f.92.33. 360 rds Expended. 60 rds fired to Support of Liverpools. Raid at Loos. RA TM Opr No3 22 rds. N14c.1.7. 10 rds. N14 c.10 rds N20 a 4.2 28 rd. N1Lc 1.2. 20 rds N20 c.q.940 22 rds N20 a.5.7. no answer of 4 rds on Fosse 5. Dugouts LTM + LTM at N27.c.9.401 N33 b.00.05. N3w c.10.70. N33 - 92.33. 12 Baty. heavies from Rest Camp at Outtersellles.	
	23 —		2nd Party proceeded to Rest Camp at Audressaltes 70 rds Expended 90 rds fired on Railway Embankment and rds. N33 - 50.90.15.N34 2.10.70 N33 a. 92.35. N33 a.92.33. 7 Reinforcements Received Brigade headquarters. 2 min. adapter into Hospital Sick. Enemy TM quiet. Balloon Broke from its Guy Ropes.	
	24—		Expended 95 rds. 60 rds on Fosse 5 and TM. N33.92.33. N33 a.90.90. 8 rds on Clog Tunnel.	
	25		Expended 142 rounds, on Fosse 5 + T.M. Postlights at N20 2.45. 55. N1Lc. 30. 6. N20 a. 9. Capt. C.A. Crusot - MC reported back from LEAVE.	
	26.		Expended 240 Rounds on different Targets. Telephone Suspension Wires Renewed	
	27		on LEAVE Expended 235 Rds. 70 rds on Dugouts at N33.f. 05.10 were in front of Embarkment N33.d. Fosse 5. 14 rds on Clog Tunnel. 12 rds on Bridge N20.d.20.46. 83 rds on TM - N20.c.82.99. N20 a 50 30	called on

Army Form C. 2118.

WAR DIARY
or
INTELLIGENCE SUMMARY.
(Erase heading not required.)

Instructions regarding War Diaries and Intelligence Summaries are contained in F.S. Regs., Part II. and the Staff Manual respectively. Title pages will be prepared in manuscript.

July 1918.

Place	Date	Hour	Summary of Events and Information	Remarks and references to Appendices
St Lucia	28.		Expended 70 rds on Hun M/Gun Emplacement at N.33 & N.33.a.4.5. N.39.a.4.9.c Fosse 5. Dugouts N.20 a.46.30. Enemy shelling Liévin	
	29.		Expended 150 Rounds 60 rounds on Huns at N.27.C.52. N.33.a.4.9. + M.T.M's at N.27.C.9.4. 5 mm. N.20.a.52.53. 5 Rds N.20.a.45.43. 5 Rds N.20.c 50.31. 5 Rds N.20.c.82.30. 5 Rds N.20.c.95.08. 30 rds on Mine N.14.c.15.05. 30 rds on H/gun N.14.c.0.3. with Good shelling	
	30.		Expended 110 Rounds. 90 rds fired on T.M Mine and Dugouts at N.33.c. N.33.a.4.9. N.33.a.4.5. N.27.C.5.2. N.27.C.9-4. 20 rds on Trench N.20.a.4.4. No casualties observed.	
	31.		Expended 180 Rds. 60 rds fired on Suspect J. successful Rds. SEE RDXX 40 rds on N.14.a.13.40. 10 rds fired on Germans in front. 70 rds on M.T.M's being removed at N.33.a. N.33.d. N.27.c. N.33.c. N.33.c.65.85. with Good shooting 11.30pm	

Crawforther Capt.
D.T.M.O. 20th Divn

1. VIII. 1918.

CONFIDENTIAL

Vol 32

War Diary
of
20th RA Trench Mortars
from 1st to 31st August 1918
Vol VIII

(6339) Wt. W160/M3016 1,500,000 10/17 McA & W Ltd (E 1898) Forms W3091.   Army Form W.3091.

Cover for Documents.

Nature of Enclosures.

Notes, or Letters written.

WAR DIARY or INTELLIGENCE SUMMARY

Army Form C. 2118.

(Erase heading not required.)

August 1918.

Place	Date	Hour	Summary of Events and Information	Remarks and references to Appendices
In the field	1.8.18		Expended 150 rds. 70 rds fired on Embankment H.T.M. Dugouts at N33.b. N33.a. 95. 85. 10 rds on Post N20.a.2.8. 40 rds on Fosse St LOUIS. 30 rds on Line N.W.205.05. Night Gas Shelling	
	2.8.18		Expended 170 rds. 100 rds on N.W.6. 15.00. to 10.15. 70 rds on Embankment August T.M. positions at N.33.a. N35.&.45. N27.c.5.2. 1 NCO. 1 Man proceeded on Conventional Course.	
	3.8.18		Expended 130 rds. 90 rds on Wire at N27 & N33.a. N33.d. 40 rds on N.W.C.1.2. 1 NCO proceeded on Gas Course. Call. TEST. Civian Carried out. Iron Civian.	
	4.8.18		Expended 135 HTR 78 rds on Wire Suspects T.M positions at N33.a. N33.a.28. 40 rds on N30 at 45.60	
	5.8.18		Expended 140 rds 60 rds on Wire Suspects at N33. A.B.D. N33.a. 9.9. 80 rds on Special Target N.W.C. 10.18.	
	6.8.18		Expended 155 rds on Wire T.M Positions at N.W.C. 2/Lieut JES Cather Hounded 1.N.C.O. 1 Man suspects b Rst Camp at Aucricagalles 1 Man Returns from Hospital 1 Man admitted into Hospital Sick	
	7.8.18		Expended 80 rds in Support of Raid Capt BOV Hoather proceed on Special French Leave. Capt. G.S.Purall. M.C. D.T.M.O. in Capt Hoather absence	
	8.8.18		Expended 140 rds on different targets Lieut K D Flatter 16 1/20 T.M.B.y. from C/91 Bde. R.F.A. 2nd poorly returns from Rst Camp 1 Man mounted into Hospital Sick Telephone Suspended.	
	9.8.18		Expended 230 rds. 40 rds on Saline & Sallon Tranches 100 rds on Were T Gilbert 70 rds on Target in support of Raid	
	10.8.18		Expended 60 rds on Wire in front Sailors & Saline & T.M positions in vicinity. Lieut J.E.S Cather struck off the Strength. D.R. R.O. 16.8.18.	
	11.8.18		Expended 110 rds on various targets	
	12.8.18		Expended 75 rds. 45 rds on Wire at N33.d.80.65. 18 rds on N.W.308.25. 6 rds. N20.a. 35.95 6 rds. N.W.C.45.25. 1 Man Returned from Leave. 9 men posted from Edn St.O.6.	
	13.8.18		Expended 70 rds. 50 rds N33.a. 80.65. 20 rds on Wire N.W.C.10.20. 1 Man proceeded on Leave, 1 Man proceeded on tour of duty in England	
	14.8.18		Expended 60 rds 20 rds on Wire at N33 a. 20.65. 20 rds on N20.a 20.95. 20 rds on different Targets 11 Men posted from 20th D.A.C.	

C.R.Ashtonton Capt.
D.T.M.O. 20th Div.

WAR DIARY
or
INTELLIGENCE SUMMARY.
(Erase heading not required.)

Army Form C. 2118.

Instructions regarding War Diaries and Intelligence Summaries are contained in F. S. Regs., Part II. and the Staff Manual respectively. Title pages will be prepared in manuscript.

Place	Date	Hour	Summary of Events and Information	Remarks and references to Appendices
	15.8.16		Expended 160 rds Bo rds on Mine at N33.d 80.65. 20 rds on N33.a 55.56. 90 Us on Mine along Embankment N14.c.16. N20.a 35.95. 2/Lieut L Johnson joint R.E. Brown died	
	16"		Expended 63 rds. 63 rds on Mine on front of Salient Sallow trenches and L.T.M's at N27@90.20. Lieut F. Hebel Smith 1/60 T.M.By. posted to V. Corps 1/20 T.M.B. Take over S.6. Newton from VIII Division 1 Man Granted Special Leave. 1 Man reported from 1/60 TM By. 16 20th B.G.R. + Man posted from 20th B.G.R. 1 Man admitted into Hospital Sick.	
	17"		Expended 115 rds. 55 rds on Mine LTMs N27 @90.2. 30 rds on N 20. a. b. 6. 47. 20 rds on N.20.a.2.9. Capt A.O.N. Heather D.T.M.O. returns from leave. 1 Man admitted into Hospital	
	18"		Expended 120 rds. 60 rds on Mine in front Sallow + Salient trenches. 60 rds N20 @ 09.52. 2 men Return from Conditional Course. 1 Man Return from Gas Course	
	19"		Expended 20 rds. 60 rds on Mine in front Salient Sallow + Hohl trenches 20 rds N14.c.3.0. 20 rds on N14.c.15.20. Capt T Neill proceeds on Special French Leave.	
	20"		Expended 135 rds - 60 rds on Mine in front Sallow Salient Hohl trenches 75 rds on Mine N14.a. 3.6. Ne Son Landed cris to 24th Division. Lieut S.G. Hayes proceeds on Leave to U.K.	
	21st		Expended 120 rounds. 60 rds on Mine in front of Sallow Salient + Hohl trenches 16 rds on N20.a 39.98. 20 rds on N20. a. N14.c.80.90. 2 men return from Cadet Camps	
	22nd		Expended 140 rds. 40 rds on target added. 60 rds on Mine Salient Sallow trenches 10 rds on N20.a 36.98. 10 rds N14.c 20.15. Remainder on Various Targets	
	23rd		Expended 80 rds 60 rds on Mine Sallow Salient + Hohl trenches. 20 rds on Various targets. 2Lieut C. Stone seconded	
	24"		Expended 60 rds 60 rds on Mine Sallow Salient trenches 1 Man proceeds on Parloune. 2 men returned from Hospital	
	25"		Expended 120 rds 50 rds on Mine trench N14.c.3.0. 10 rds on T.M's @ N20. b.85-56. 60 rds on Line in front Sallow + Salient trenches + H.T.M's @ N33.b.10.68. 1 man admitted into Hospital Sick	
	26"		Expended 120 rds. 65 on Mine in front Salient Sallow Hohl trenches Fosse 4. 50 rds on Mine a N20.a. 4.8.15 N20.a.30.15. + N14.c.5.0.	
	27"		Expended 135 rds. 20 rds on Mine + MGs at N27.a 15.20. 15 rds @ N14.C.5.0. N14.c 15.12. 15 rds N14.c 10.39. 15 rds N14.c.00.35. 75 rds fired on Support of Raid. 2 men return from Hospital	

Capt A.O.N. Heather D.T.M.O. 20th Divn.

Army Form C. 2118.

WAR DIARY
or
INTELLIGENCE SUMMARY.
(Erase heading not required.)

Instructions regarding War Diaries and Intelligence Summaries are contained in F. S. Regs., Part II. and the Staff Manual respectively. Title pages will be prepared in manuscript.

Place	Date	Hour	Summary of Events and Information	Remarks and references to Appendices
	28.8.18		Expended 100 Rds .75.Rds on MGS @ N27 a 1.2 47Ms @ N27 a, 7.2, + 47Ms @ N33.6 6.3. Cpl. J. Neill returns from Special Leave. Lieut. Kendall takes over New Section from 8th Division	
	29.8.18		Expended 70 Rds on Railway Embankment from N33 b 2.5 to N33 a 9.8. 3.6 "Newton" + 1273 Rds of Ammunition taken over to the 2nd Division. 375 Rds of Ammunition taken over from the 8th Division	
	30.8.18		Expended 70 Rds. 70 Rds fired Wilkins pattern M.G.T. and Embankment. 1/30 T M Bty take over the Section @ Nielers	
	31.8.18		Expended 72 Rds . 72 Rds fired on Wire in front Sailly Maillet Saline Trenches + M G @ N.27 C.8. 5.	

(signed) Capt
DTMO [illegible]

CONFIDENTIAL

Vol 33

War Diary
of
30th T.A. Trench Mortars

from 1st to 30th Sept 1918

Vol IX

(6339) Wt. W160/M3016 1,500,000 10/17 McA & W Ltd (E 1898) Forms W3091.　　Army Form W.3091.

Cover for Documents.

Nature of Enclosures.

Notes, or Letters written.

WAR DIARY or INTELLIGENCE SUMMARY

Army Form C. 2118.

1917

Place	Date	Hour	Summary of Events and Information	Remarks and references to Appendices
	1.9.17		Expended 80 rds on Wire in front Embankment Sallar Sallar Trenches	
	2nd		Nothing of note. 1 Man admitted into hospital	
	3rd		Expended 80 rds 80 rds behind Embankment from N.27.B.90.30. N.27.a.90.60. and Trenches in N.22.a	
	4th		Expended 48 rds 48 rds on Wire @ N.27.C.R.40. N.33.b.50.35. in conjunction with Artillery	
			Lt. Munro Moved Bde Headquarters moved from Tillenceux to Le Touquet. 1 Man admitted into hospital. Sick	
	5th		Expended 70 rds 70 rds on Embankment @ N.27.b and C. One Off. & Emit proceeds on Leave	
			Lieut. J.G. Hayes. Returns from Leave. 1 Man Wins from Leave. 1 L/C Menton and 1 OS Bowes	
			Relieved by Enemy's Shell Fire. 5 Men admitted into hospital	
	6th		Expended 120 rds 120 rds fired on Mine being embankment N.27.F. N.33.a. N.33.F. N.34.C	
	7th		Expended 130 rds on Wire behind Embankment and at Tk. Trenches. Opera & N.27.a. & N.33 b-b	
			N.33.c. 1 Man admitted into hospital	
	8th		Expended 100 rds 100 rds Harassing fire behind Embankment and on Trenches N.33 & N.34.F	
			N.33.b. 1 NCO admitted into hospital	
	9th		Expended 125 rds. 100 rds on Wire in front of Embankment N.27.d. N.33.b & 10. N.34.C.25 Rds	
			on Wire at N.34.C.7.3. 1 Man transferred to Leave	
	10th		Expended 50 rds on Wire in front of Embankment N.27.c and N.27.a. 7.4.a.80.80. 6 T u.a. 10.75.	
	11th		Expended 100 rds 70 rds on Wire in N.33.d. and N.34.c & 30 rds. 7.4.a.80.00	
	12th		General intercourse 27.NO. at 202 320 1917 on N.27.d and N.34.c also wires in N.33.d & N.27.C	
	13th		Expended 125 rds. 105 rds on Wire in N.27.d and N.34.c and N.33.d. Suspect air movement 15 T. NO.	
	14th		Expended 100 rds. 100 rds on Wire N.27.c. N.33.a N.33.a N.34.c Lieut Hollow to 1 Man	
			at Brigade HQrs	
	15th		Expended 140 rds 100 rds on Wire on Hoodles.	
			Proceed to 1st Army School of Musketry	
	16th		Expended 100 rds on suspecting Targets N.27.b. N.33.a N.33.a. N.33.b.60.14 Wire position C.91 Bde	
	17th		Expended 230 rds on Wire – N.27. N.33.a N.33.a. N.33.b.60. 16 N.33.b.20.30. 7.4.a.3.5 Ammunity	
			Expended 150 rds on Wire in N.27. N.38.a. N.33.b.60.16 N.33.b.7.0. 6 N.33.b. 20.30. N.34.a.	
			1 Man admitted into Hospital Sick	
	18th		Expended 120 rds on Wire in N.27b. N.33.a+b. N.33 A 7.0. & N.33+ 20.30. N.34.a.	
			7.4.a. 3.5. 6 T 1 Mounty	H.M. Marshall Lt R.F.A.

WAR DIARY
or
INTELLIGENCE SUMMARY.
(Erase heading not required.)

Army Form C. 2118.

September 1918

Place	Date	Hour	Summary of Events and Information	Remarks and references to Appendices
	19.9.18		Enemy Post taken in Line in N27c. N33a+b. N34.d. N33.b.c.c. & N33.d. 20.30. T.H.a.	
	20.9.18		Exposed 150 rds on Line in N27c. N33a.t.b. T.H.a. May arrival 225 NCO admitted to Sick. C.S.M. Jones M.C. returned from leave in England.	
	21.9.18		Excursion 30 rds on Line in N27c. N33d. N33b. T.H.a. Col. J. Neil proceeded Leave to England.	
	22.9.18		Excursion 100 rds on Line. INCO returned from hospital. Maj. Brown on Leave.	
			Line Emplacements Tongnets in N33b. N33c. N27c. N279.9.3.	
	23.9.18		N33.b. 05.70. N35.b.5.2. INCO wounded.	
			Enemy 174 rds on Line. Supports + Movements behind enemy Front in	
			N33.a.b. N27c. N33.b.8.3. N27c. P.2. Our men fired in Support + Infantry	
	24.9.18		Exposed 170. 150 rds fired on Line in N53 arb. N27c. Enemy's Emplacement KRuins	
			Embankment at N33. t.5.5. N275.8.2. N27c.8.5. 20 rds + Support + Field	
	25.9.18		Excursion 140. 8rd. Wire in N33d. Belief Enlistment. N27c.8.5.16. N27c-5.5.	
			dugouts at N33.b. 05.70. MG.7 Turnback in T.H.b. 52.48. T.H.b. 05.50. Wire Transfered	
			9th/Bev. Telephone to Wagon Line Completed.	
	26.9.18		Excursion 160 rds on Trenches T.H.b. 50.45. to T.H.b. 50.70. T.H.b. 05.50. Support N33.b. 10.70.	
			Embankment N275. 1. 16 N27c 8.5.	Enlistment Completed
	27.9.18		Excursion 170 rds Embankment N27c.8.1.b. N27c.8.5. 100 pound N34.a.2.E. N34.c.53.13.	
			at N33f 05.70. N33.b.05.10. MG. in N33.a.1.7. Line in N33.a. T.H.a.2.E. N34.c.53.13.	
	28.9.18		Excursion 200 rds on Embankment N27c.8.1.b. N27c.8.5. Line in Swallow Trench	Swallow Trench
			Sergeants N33b 05.70. N33.b.5.2. MG.7. T.H.b.6.25.50. T.H.a.50.55. First Entered
			Transferred to R.A.F. Proceeded to England.	
	29.9.18		Excursion 140 rds Wire in Honor at N27c.25.05. dugout N27c.15.20. N27c.90.45.	
			MG.7. Railway N27c95.70. Post H. Line in T.H.a.O.F.b. T.H.a.4.C. T.H.a. 80.55	
			2/Lieut. R.C. Brown Proceeds to 1st Army School of Machines.	
	30.9.18		Excursion 105 rds on Honor Tongnets N27a. T.36.80.95. T.H.a.3.7. N33.T. 70.15.	
			16.T.H.a. 20.95. Line in N33.a. 2/Lt. K.D. Parker relieved from 1st Army School of	
			Motors 21.9.18. Newton out of action	H.L.Kendrick, Lt. R.A.

Confidential

Vol 34

War Diary
of
20th RA Trench Mortars.
from 1st to 31st October 1918
Vol X

(6339) Wt. W160/M3016 1,500,000 10/17 McA & W Ltd (E 1898) Forms W3091.   Army Form W.3091.

Cover for Documents.

Nature of Enclosures.

Notes, or Letters written.

Army Form C. 2118.

WAR DIARY
or
INTELLIGENCE SUMMARY.
(Erase heading not required.)

Oct. 1918

Place	Date	Hour	Summary of Events and Information	Remarks and references to Appendices
	1.10.18		Extended H.Q. was at Trenches in N 31. C.10.75. N 31. C. 68.40. behind Embankment N 33 d 85.90. 1 Nr. Proceeds on Colour Course at Auchesvilles.	
	2.10.18		No reconnaissance or patrols out.	
	3.10.18		Lieut. Kendall Excoyen & Newtons from 8th Divisional Trench Mortar.	
	4.10.18		Nothing else to report.	
	5.10.18		1 Man proceed on Leave. Corpl. Funnie Killed in Action. Sergt. Junch wounded at La Targelle.	
	6.10.18		German Trails Wagon Lines.	
	7.10.18		Havas Trench Mortar Positions 6.50% Divisional Trench Mortar Bde.	
	8.10.18		Bdo Moves Off from La Targelle to Moreuil. 1 Man proceeds on leave. 1st Army Reinforcement Camp.	
	9.10.18		Lieut. L.O. Hosker proceeds on Leave. 1 Man posted from 1st Army Reinforcement Camp.	
		6/7.0 T.M. Bty	Baggage Wagons & from Moreuil to Thievres by Motor Lorries Corpl. I. Cor. D.C.M. + 60 T.M. Bty promoted Sergt.	
	10.10		General Inspection of the Brigade by D.B.T.M.O.	
	11.10		General Conference D.T.M.O. at Thievry.	
	12./.		E.S. Lyons proceeds on leave to England. Brigade on strike in Mobile Mortar Warfare.	
	13.10		Lieut. movements D.T.M.O. at Chevrey. Lieut R.C. Brown returns from T.M. Reece.	
	14.10		General movements of Mobile Mortar Batteries. 1 Sergt. proceeds on leave.	
	15.10		Brigade instruction in Mobile Mortar Warfare	
	16.10		Very quiet.	
	17.10		Mobile Mortar Wagons instruction 1 Man proceeds on leave.	
	18./.		Exchanging Camps. Salvaging	
	19.10		Salvaging	
	20.10		Mobile Mortar Warfare instruction & Salvaging.	
	21.1.		"	
	22 nd		1 Man proceeds on leave.	

Comdg. B.J.A. Trench Mortars
20th Divisn.

Army Form C. 2118.

WAR DIARY
or
INTELLIGENCE SUMMARY.
(Erase heading not required.)

Oct 1917.

Instructions regarding War Diaries and Intelligence Summaries are contained in F. S. Regs., Part II. and the Staff Manual respectively. Title pages will be prepared in manuscript.

Place	Date	Hour	Summary of Events and Information	Remarks and references to Appendices
Salvaging	23.10.17		Capt A.A.V. Hooper proceeds on leave.	
	24.		NCO proceeds on leave, 1 Salvaging	
	25.		General Duties. Capt G.G Grant M.C.	
	26.		and K.10 Station returns from leave	
	27.		1 man proceeds on leave. Salvaging	
	28.		" " Road repairing party E.S. Steam Retain tent.	
	29.		Warned to proceed 6.am the 30th Coyd	
	30.		proceeded 6am the 8th Army. 1 Man ordered on leave	
	31.		Clernay to Cambrai in meantime to report from Cambrai	

G.G. Grant Capt.
Comdg. R.A. Lunch Mortars.
20th Division.

CONFIDENTIAL.

War Diary

of

20th. Divnl. Arty. Trench Mortars.

From 1.11.18 to 30.11.18.

Vol: XI.

(6392) Wt. W6192/P875 1,500,000   4/18   McA & W Ltd (E 2815)   Forms W3091/4.   Army Form W.3091.

Cover for Documents.

Nature of Enclosures.

Notes, or Letters written.

Army Form C. 2118.

WAR DIARY
or
INTELLIGENCE SUMMARY. November 1918.
(Erase heading not required.)

Instructions regarding War Diaries and Intelligence Summaries are contained in F. S. Regs., Part II, and the Staff Manual respectively. Title pages will be prepared in manuscript.

Place	Date	Hour	Summary of Events and Information	Remarks and references to Appendices
In the Field	1.11.18.		Billeted at Lambrai. Awaiting Orders to proceed forward	
	2.		Received Orders to Move from Lambrai to Mountrecourt	
	3.		Moved from Mountrecourt to Verchain. 2 Men proceed on Leave.	
	4.		Still at Verchain 40 NCOs+Men attached to 91st+92nd Bdes R.F.A. for duty.	
	5.		20 NCOs attached 204 B.A.C. for duty. 1 Man proceeds on Leave. 1 Man admitted into Hospital Sick	
	6.		Moved from Verchain to Jenlain. 2 Men proceed on Leave.	
	7th		Lieut H.J.L Kendall x/to T.M.Bty. proceeds on Leave. 1 NCO proceeds on Leave (2 Men wounded Gassed whilst attached to 92nd Bde R.F.A.)	
	8th		Moved from Jenlain to Bavgnies Le Grand	
	9th		Moved " Bavgnies Le Grand to Hamengrie 1 Man proceeds on Leave	
	10th		Moved " Hamengrie to Bellignies 1 Man wounded 1 NCO killed in Action whilst attached to 92nd Bde R.F.A. 1 Man proceeds on Leave	
	11th		Hostilities Ceased	
	12th		NCO + Men return from T.M. Course.	
	13th		Party of French Mortar Personnel Bury 3 Men of Yorkshire Regt. killed in Action	
	14th		Capt A.O.V. Heather (B.T.M.O. repairs unit) from Leave in England	
	15th		2 Men proceed on Leave	

WAR DIARY
or
INTELLIGENCE SUMMARY.
(Erase heading not required.)

Army Form C. 2118.

Instructions regarding War Diaries and Intelligence Summaries are contained in F. S. Regs., Part II. and the Staff Manual respectively. Title pages will be prepared in manuscript.

Place	Date	Hour	Summary of Events and Information	Remarks and references to Appendices
	16.11.18.		1 Man proceeds on Leave	
	17th		1 " proceeds on Leave	
	18th		Nil	
	19th		2 men return limit from Leave. 1 Man proceeds on Leave.	
	20th		Lot. Ew. comes into Belligines. Football match v/ult K.R.R.	
	21st		Awaiting Orders to move.	
	22nd		Moved from Belligines to Orsinval by own Transport	
	23rd		2 G.S. wagons returns to Belligines for remainder of Stores	
	24th		Moved from Orsinval to Tambrai	
	25th		Nil	
	26th		Received Orders to move. 2 Men proceed on Leave	
	27th		Moved from Tambrai to HERU. 3 Officers 21 O.R. entrained remainder by Transport. Staying at Beaurepaire for night	
	28th		Moved off from Beaurepaire to HERU	
	29th		Nil	
	30th		NCOs & Men report from Art. Bde. 240 Bde R.F.A.	

Vol 36

"Confidential"

War Diary
of
20th Divnl. Aty. Trench Mortars.

From 1:12:18. To 31:12:18.

Vol: 12.

(6392) Wt. W6192/P875 1,500,000 4/18 McA & W Ltd (E 2815) Forms W3091/4.   Army Form W.3091.

Cover for Documents.

Nature of Enclosures.

Notes, or Letters written.

WAR DIARY
or
INTELLIGENCE SUMMARY.
(Erase heading not required.)

Army Form C. 2118.

December 1918

Place	Date	Hour	Summary of Events and Information	Remarks and references to Appendices
In the Field	1.12.18		Capt. Neill, 2nd in Command, returns from Cambrai, leaving the Train Party "locally".	a.a.a.
	2.		Train Party arrives at Henin. 2 Men proceed on leave to England.	a.a.a.
	3.		One Man proceeds on leave to England.	a.a.a.
	6.		Brigade Football Team beats A/91 Bde. R.F.A. result 2-2.	a.a.a.
	7.		Brigade Football Team beats B/91 in League.	a.a.a.
	8.		Proceeded to bring back Gun Stores from Arras. Capt. Feather & T.M.O. to England.	a.a.a.
			In charge of Party & Lorries. Education Class in French Schoolroom.	a.a.a.
	9.		Party return from Arras with Gun Stores. League Football Match. C/91 Bde. R.A. beat	a.a.a.
			The Miner proceeds to England. Lecture by Capt. Neill.	a.a.a.
	14.		League Football Match with 19/91. 106 R.F.A. at La Herlière.	a.a.a.
	15.		Capt. C.L. Evans, M.C. reports sick	a.a.a.
	16.			a.a.a.
	17.		NCO's & Men return to Unit from 9th. Bn. R.F.O. Lieut Alder lectures on Henri Schotmansloo.	a.a.a.
	18.		Two Men report sick. 1 Man returns to Unit from 92 Bn. R.F.O. Germany to 91 R.F.O.	a.a.a.
	19.		One Man transferred to B/92 Bde. R.F.O. One Man transferred from B/92 Bn. R.F.O.	a.a.a.
	20.		General brushes inspects Camp	a.a.a.
	21.		NCO & Men return to Unit from 92 Bde R.F.O.	Capt.

Capt. North
R.A. Trench Mortars,
20th Division.

WAR DIARY or INTELLIGENCE SUMMARY.

Army Form C. 2118.

(Erase heading not required.)

Place	Date	Hour	Summary of Events and Information	Remarks and references to Appendices
In the Field	23		Lieut L.G. Hayes 1/70 T.M. Bty. proceeds to Abbeville on Fuel Course.	auth
			3 Miners proceed to England.	auth
	25.		Berullias Day. Brigade at Dinner.	auth
	27		Lieut R.C. Brown 1/70 T.M. Bty. proceeds on Educational course	auth
	29		League football final with Afz. Bde R.F.A.	auth
	30.		Three Miners proceed to England. League football match visit 102 the Bde.	auth
	31st		Board of Enquiry (Capt. J. Neill, President) Three Men return from Leave.	auth

A.W. Heaton
Capt
DTMO 20th Divn.

Comdg. R.A. Trench Mortars.
20th Division.

War Diary

of

20th Divnl. Arty Trench Mortars.

From: 1st Jan. 1919.
To: 31st Jan. 1919.

Vol: I.

(6392) Wt. W6192/P875 1,500,000 4/18 McA & W Ltd (E 2815) Forms W3091/4. Army Form W.3091.

Cover for Documents.

Nature of Enclosures.

Notes, or Letters written.

WAR DIARY or INTELLIGENCE SUMMARY.

Army Form C. 2118.

January 1919

Place	Date	Hour	Summary of Events and Information	Remarks and references to Appendices
In the Field	1		2nd Lieut. J.G. Hayes reported back from French leave.	19.4
	2		1 Man reported back from leave.	19.4
			Capt. A.O.V. Leather. 1st Royal Berks D.T.M.O. interviews O.C. 6. Division	29.4
			reported back from leave.	
	3		Capt. E.J. Grant. M.C. and Capt. J. Gill R.G.A. 1st C.S.O. and 2 Men	19.4
			proceeded on course of gunnery to 3rd Army Artillery School	
	4		Capt. A.O.V. Leather. 1st Royal Berks D.T.M.O. interviews O.C.D.	19.4
			2 Men report sick	
	5		2 Men proceed to England on leave 1 Man reported	19.4
			back from leave	
	6		2 Men hrd for leave without absence.	19.4
	7			19.4
	8		Football match D/94 G.S.O. versus Th. Bde. unit 8/94 3 Th. Bde. 1	19.4
			1 Man proceeds on leave.	
	9		O.C. G.O. interviews Capt. A.O.V. Leather D.T.M.O.	19.4
	10		2/Lt. Johnson proceeds on leave Football Match. Hd. D.A.C. 6. Th. Bde. 0.	19.4

L.A. Hayes 2/Lt
for D.T.M.O.

Army Form C. 2118.

WAR DIARY
or
INTELLIGENCE SUMMARY.
(Erase heading not required.)

January 1919

Place	Date	Hour	Summary of Events and Information	Remarks and references to Appendices
M.R. Sub	11		1 Man proceeds on leave	App
	12		1 O.R. & O.R. proceed on Education Course. 17th Corps School. 3 Men proceed to England demobilized	App
	14		1 Man proceeds to England demobilized. Football Match 3 Lec DAC versus TMBn result D.O.C. 2 T.M.Bn ch.	App
	15		1 Man proceeds to England demobilized. 6 Officers stragglers report back	App
	16		Football Match 1 Coy Div Train versus TMBn result 1 Coy 1 T.M.0	App
	17		1 Man reports back from leave. 4 Officers unwounds	App
	18		1 Man proceeds on leave. 1 Man proceeds to England demobilized	App
	19		1 Man proceeds to England demobilized	App
	20		1 Man reports back from leave. 1 return reported Sick.	App
	21		1 Man proceeds to England on leave.	App
	22		1 Man reported sick.	App
	23		G.O.C visits	App

L.Ahaye 2/Lt M.V.
for B.T.M.O.

Army Form C. 2118.

WAR DIARY
or
INTELLIGENCE SUMMARY.
(Erase heading not required.)

January 1919

Place	Date	Hour	Summary of Events and Information	Remarks and references to Appendices
In the Field	25		4 Other proceed to England demobilised	194
	26		3 " " " " "	
			England on leave 2/Lt Flasher takes charge of horse guns	
			outer from B/yo	
	27		Capt J A Heather continues Bde Major.	194
	28		1 M Bde dislocated Capt A.W. Wollen & 2/Lt Kendall proceed to	194
			No 2 Sec 9 DAC with all guns and equipment	
	30		Capt A.W. Wollen proceeds on leave in France 2/Lt Kendall	194
			transferred to No 2 Sec 20th DAC	
	28		Capt E S Heard + 2/Lt S G Lyon proto to 91st Bde RGA	194
			Capt J Neill 2/Lt S K Hayes 2/Lt F D Flasher 2/Lt R C Brown + 2/Lt	
			F Wilson proto to 92nd Bde RGA	194
			All S.N. personnel distributed among units in 20" Div Arty	

S.N. Hayes
Lt R.F.A.
For O.C. T.M.O.

WR 36
Cersed

War Diary
of
20th Divnl. Ortry. Trench Mortars.

From: 1:2:19.
To: 28:2:19.

Vol: 2.

CONFIDENTIAL

(6392) Wt. W6192/P875 1,500,000 4/18 McA & W Ltd (**E 2815**) Forms W3091/4.   Army Form W.3091.

Cover for Documents.

Nature of Enclosures.

Notes, or Letters written.

WAR DIARY
or
INTELLIGENCE SUMMARY.

February 1919

(Erase heading not required.)

Instructions regarding War Diaries and Intelligence Summaries are contained in F. S. Regs., Part II. and the Staff Manual respectively. Title pages will be prepared in manuscript.

Place	Date	Hour	Summary of Events and Information	Remarks and references to Appendices
			Owing to Trench Mortars having been disbanded on 28.1.19 and all men gone to different Brigades nothing is recorded during present month	Capt

Cavillather
Capt.
Comdg. R. A. Trench Mortars,
20th Division.

www.ingramcontent.com/pod-product-compliance
Lightning Source LLC
Chambersburg PA
CBHW081409160426
43193CB00013B/2139